Oh yes, oh yes!

Oh yes, oh yes!

CARL COX

with Alon Shulman

WHITE
RABBIT

First published in Great Britain in 2021 by White Rabbit,
an imprint of The Orion Publishing Group Ltd
Carmelite House, 50 Victoria Embankment
London EC4Y 0DZ

An Hachette UK Company

1 3 5 7 9 10 8 6 4 2

A CIP catalogue record for this book is
available from the British Library.

ISBN (Hardback) 978 1 4746 1627 0
ISBN (Export Trade Paperback) 978 1 4746 1629 4
ISBN (eBook) 978 1 4746 1631 7
ISBN (Audio) 978 1 4746 1632 4

Typeset by Born Group
Printed and bound in Great Britain by Clays Ltd, Elcograf S.p.A.

MIX
Paper from
responsible sources
FSC® C104740

www.whiterabbitbooks.co.uk
www.orionbooks.co.uk

Contents

The King

BY ALON SHULMAN

Carl Cox, the Three Deck Wizard, is a living legend. Instrumental in the birth of the dance music scene and club culture, he continues to be at the forefront of the global dance music industry. He has music pumping through his veins and exudes an almost superhuman electrical energy wherever he goes. His whole mission is about spreading the joy that he gets from music to all of us. Once you've been to a Carl Cox gig and been initiated there's no going back. You're hooked.

For those of us lucky enough to work alongside Carl, be it on stage, in the studio or at the track, it is clear why he generates so much admiration from his peers. His determination to succeed and to be the very best he can be is what drives him forward, but everything he does involves a deep consideration for the industry that he has helped to shape and that he loves so much. Hugely respected by artists and fans alike, Coxy never seems to slow down, continuing to push himself to greater heights.

Few have been able to match the dedication and passion that Carl brings to his performances. His attitude, enthusiasm and passion, coupled with his incredible feeling for music, is what makes him so special. The almost magical aura that surrounds him is what makes him the DJ's DJ. His technical mastery and musical selection puts him on a pedestal. But it is the way he openly shares his heart and soul with us that makes him unique. He really is the absolute greatest at what he does, and we love him for it. All hail the King!

Alon Shulman,
London 2021

'Nobody in dance music works harder than Carl Cox. He's always pushing himself to achieve more and more and that's what propelled him to global superstardom. His command of the dancefloor is next level.'
Paul Oakenfold

'Carl simply claims the stage by just being himself: a no-nonsense, uplifting spirit that lights up every room. Out of all the DJs out there he has always been the one I look up to.'
Ferry Corsten

'Carl Cox is the King of Clubs and also the King of Streams. He's a very dear friend and a mentor who for over thirty years has never ceased to inspire me. There are not enough words to describe this living legend. I love him to bits.'
Nicole Moudaber

'After meeting Carl on so many occasions he still makes you feel comfortable every single time and is genuinely interested in what people are doing and what they have to say. He has been a top professional now for over thirty years and is still an inspiration to many, including myself. He is the ultimate role model that every young DJ should aspire to be. What else can you say? There will never be another Carl . . .'
Adam Beyer

'Carl is like the gold standard of DJing. For the twenty-five years or so I've watched him DJ he has never faltered in his passion for quality music, dedication to his art and endless work ethic. He has led the way and achieved everything there is to achieve all while remaining truly humble. I didn't know Carl thirty-plus years ago when he was starting out but I imagine it's the same Carl you would meet today. He's the legend of legends.'
Jamie Jones

'Carl Cox wrote the script of what it means to be a DJ. He's led the dance for decades and created a global underground movement that became the blueprint for the festivals and tours that followed for us all. His innate sense of what makes people connect to music is a gift. But this isn't just a story of *what* he achieved, it's *how*. Carl's passion, determination and imagination are just as legendary as his talent and the *joie de vivre* he brings to the party. It's a tale about being relentless against the odds, with a vision and a purpose. His story should inspire the next generation of DJs, party people and music makers and remind us of what we can create when we come together.'
David Guetta

'Carl always had something special about him. He had that X factor. The memory that sticks out was when we were at a rave in Milton Keynes and all the lads were playing - Bryan Gee, Carl, Jumping Jack Frost, Grooverider and me. There I was sitting down with Carl listening to Grooverider. Groove was killing it. Carl turned round to me and said, "I'm going to start playing techno, that's it for me." We were all playing hardcore/ jungle in the early days. I nudged him and said, "Why, are you

crazy?" "I don't know one track Groove has played, I'm just not getting the tunes, I'm gonna try something else," he replied. It was a brave move. One that I thought would be hard to pull off. The rest is history. No need to explain what happened next. Carl is the DJs' DJ. He has the passion, skill and energy. I'm not surprised at all that he became one of the greatest of all time. On top of everything he is such a warm and gentle person and deserves every bit of success that has come his way.'
Fabio

'Carl has always been my favourite. He is the complete DJ, also the DJs' DJ. Records come to life when he plays them, rooms come to life when he rocks them. His enthusiasm is infectious, his commitment complete.'
Norman Cook aka Fatboy Slim

'From the early days of rave, Sterns in Worthing, the Astoria, Club UK, the End, to him playing for us at our Shake It warehouse parties and me for him at Space Ibiza, we have had a million magic moments together. Carl is one of the warmest, most generous, most charismatic people I have ever met. He is at the very top of his game and always has been. His talent, drive, energy and enthusiasm are next level. He is one of the most inspiring, positive, gifted DJs I have ever heard, and someone I regard as a legend, a mentor and a really special friend for life.'
Matthew Benjamin aka Bushwacka

'Carl Cox is one of the most genuine people I know. From the start, many years ago, he always greeted me with the warmest smile. You can feel he's a kind soul who just breathes music. He

is an example to all of us and a great source of inspiration. Carl is a true legend.'
Charlotte de Witte

'Carl is a true inspiration to me as a DJ but more importantly as a man. He's my favourite DJ on the planet and has been since I first watched him play in 1995. He's always been the number one and will be until he hangs up his headphones, which I hope is a long way off. Long live Carl Cox.'
Eats Everything

'I first heard Carl DJ when I was eighteen years old in a club in Streatham called Ziggy's. He was easily the most gifted DJ I'd heard from that era and was also inspiring to me as a young black youth. Who would have known many years later I'd be sharing many a stage with him. I don't think there are many people who have actually inspired me in music and DJing like Carl. I can categorically say if there wasn't a Carl Cox there would have never been a Grooverider, and to this day I don't think he realises the influence he has had on me and so many others. People use the term legend far too easily for my liking but Carl is legend personified. Thank you, Carl.'
Grooverider

'The first time I ever heard a tune that I'd made played out in a club was January 1991 in Busby's - Astoria 2 - in London. Me and the boys were having a night out, I suddenly heard "Everybody in the Place" being mixed in and I was buzzing, so I made my way through the crowd to the DJ and it was Carl playing it. I shook his hand and bounced off. That was a big moment for me as I had been to many raves in '89 and '90, standing in the

crowd listening to him play, and him playing our tune gave it a stamp of authority from the underground. Almost exactly the same thing happened when we were having another night out in London in 1996. I heard the "Firestarter" instrumental bang out the system, I made my way over to the decks and it was Carl. Tunes being played on nights out partying always create those special memories that we never forget – I know Carl was responsible for a lot of mine. Carl has always supported the Prodigy from the start and I have nothing but love and the highest respect for him, not only for his mixing ability (three turntables ol skool, i was there!), tune-making ability, passion and energy, but also for being a top geezer. No sell-out!'
Liam Howlett, the Prodigy

'Having Carl as a friend is a great privilege for me. Carl is an amazing human being and his presence in my life makes everything better, in both artistic and personal ways. I owe him a lot for all the tips and advice he gave me throughout the years. He helped me to grow and improve myself in so many ways. I'm truly honoured to be able to call him a close friend of mine. I will thank him forever for everything he has done and is still doing for me.'
Joseph Capriati

'No matter how big he's become as a DJ he has remained true to his original pioneering underground spirit. Carl is not like most underground DJs. He can play anything to anyone anywhere and make something special happen.'
Laurent Garnier

'From the moment I first heard Carl as a teenager at Checkpoint Charlie in Reading in the 1990s he has been a huge inspiration

and influence to me. I am hugely grateful for the support he has given me as an artist and the belief he has shown in what I do. His diversity as a DJ shows his undying love for music and his natural ability as a live artist is a testament to how extraordinarily talented he is. Absolute legend!'
Saytek

'Carl Cox is a timeless master DJ with a seemingly endless passion for music and DJing. I first became aware of Carl back in 1991, when he released "I Want You", which quickly became my favourite track of that era. A few years later Carl released the *F.A.C.T.* album, which remains one of my favourite albums of all time. Carl's influence on the world of electronic dance music, as a DJ, producer and businessman, cannot be overstated. He has blazed a trail for so many of us. His love for performing and genuine enthusiasm for his craft shines through on his smiling face and inspires joy in everyone around him.'
Tiësto

'Not a lot of people know this, but when I was an underage DJ and playing in a wine bar in Sutton called Christie's, it was Carl Cox who used to take over for the final thirty minutes to give me time to get home and get up for school the next day. Carl has probably forgotten this, however I haven't, and I've followed his incredible career ever since. Carl is one of the few true pioneers of UK club culture internationally. He has opened the door to so many DJs and inspired so many, including me. I have been honoured to be invited to play with him in Ibiza over the years. He is a great teacher.'
Gilles Peterson

'Carl is the master when it comes to commandeering a dance-floor. I have so much respect for that guy.'
DeadMau5

'Carl's name is synonymous with dance and club culture. He is a founding father, icon and legend, who remains as committed, joyful and passionate today as when I met him running sound systems in the 1980s. This book will further stamp his legacy in the history books and no doubt provide inspiration for future generations.'
Pete Tong MBE

'Already in the 1990s when I was a hip-hop kid I heard of Carl Cox. I met him years later, in 2003, in Ibiza on the legendary Circoloco Space Terrace. From that day Carl and I are friends. We became a tag team at Space Closing for almost four years, and it was a team play that I enjoyed the most. Proper old-school vinyl competition: Carl would play a record and I'd try to find something equally good, better, weirder. You play this? Ah, OK! Wait until you hear this one! Carl Cox is the daddy of all electronic music. His love, knowledge and passion are contagious, and he motivates us all, shows us that even a daddy can kick your ass and stay on top in times of social media and short attention span of many people. Everybody loves Carl, and I am happy that I can call him family.'
Loco Dice

'Carl is the most open-minded DJ. Musically he is a trendsetter and doesn't follow in anyone's footsteps. His passion extends to the people around him – he always wants his friends and fellow DJs to get the best out of every situation. He'd have us all

staying at the villa in Ibiza so by the time we came to the club we were part of his family and could focus on the music. He always thinks of the night as a whole rather than just focuses on his set like so many of the big artists. You couldn't ask for a better friend. I was in Australia on tour and met up with Carl and told him I wanted to see a kangaroo. No problem, he says. He drove me out to where there would be wild kangaroos and waited for an hour until one came along. Always thinking of others, that's Carl for you - big heart, big sound and big smile.'
Monika Kruse

'An event with Carl Cox is a guaranteed roadblock and his consistency behind the decks means he turns up every time and smashes it with his unmatched stage presence and positivity that just spreads through the crowd, whipping them into a frenzy night after night. He's a joy to watch and a joy to be around.'
John Digweed

'I've known Carl Cox for many years and we've experienced many great events together. Carl's a great DJ, one of the best in history. He knows how to connect with the crowd. He's a great person with a great personality and is a bunch of fun.'
Kevin Saunderson

'I first met Carl back in 1987 when he was supplying a sound system for an Essex warehouse party. I couldn't have imagined that we'd go on to be on the same line-ups at parties and festivals all over the world. He's a great a friend, a true gent and a huge inspiration to everyone. He's a true master of his craft and a wonderful human being. I love him for it.'
Darren Emerson

'Working closely with Carl in the studio over the years has taught me a lot about being decisive, positive and creative, as he embraces new technology and ideas enthusiastically. As a producer, Carl is open and intuitive and his ear for tuning, EQ and timing is spot on. He never stops searching for the perfect beat. He has an irrepressible attitude of positivity at all times. Once he gave me a simple piece of advice when going out live: "Enjoy yourself and smile a lot." This sums him up as an artist and as a friend - whenever he walks on stage, the crowd just lifts because of his big smile, his generosity and all enveloping warmth.'
Christopher Coe

'The thing I admire most in Carl, besides his love for music, beyond any reasonable doubt, is his versatility. It's captivating . . . especially when you can draw from all languages or musical styles and you choose to create your own. Then you know that you really are great, but that's what it means to be Carl Cox.'
Deborah De Luca

'I remember walking behind Carl going into an outside daytime rave in Scotland in the early 1990s. For some reason we were walking past a huge line-up of ravers trying to get into the party and suddenly people spotted Carl. Events were not so organised back then, and everyone started cheering and chanting "COXY COXY COXY!" I had never witnessed the "superstar" DJ phenomenon at that point - actually it didn't really exist still at that point - but there it was in front of me. The roar of the crowd was thundering, people loved him, and Carl took it just like he would today, in his stride, smiling, waving and high-fiving his fans as he walked by. Carl's love of music and

his fans and his humility paved the way for his success, and is something that all aspiring DJs can learn from.'
Richie Hawtin

'Carl's always been such an inspiration to me, from the early rave days being the original three deck master, to watching him totally smash down Space Ibiza time after time, to seeing him play a drum and bass set on tour in Australia and then DJ all night to all the touring crew, just for the fun of it. His talent, energy and passion for making people dance is untouchable. I've been lucky enough to be invited to play with Carl, including in Ibiza, for which I'm eternally grateful. Feeling the vibe and anticipation as he stepped into the booth was something to behold . . . truly special. His *Cabin Fever* sets just show the pure passion and dedication of the man to his music and his craft. No stone has been left unturned, a testament to his vibe that good music is good music, no matter what the style. To say this man loves his music is an understatement. I love this guy, and it's always an absolute pleasure to bump into him around the world for a catch-up and to get his advice. Plus, I get to see him smash it up again and again!'
Andy C

'The legend that is Carl Cox – a super-talented DJ with mad technical skills. Always humble, he's a beautiful human being who's loved and respected worldwide. Carl's love and passion for music always shines through. I have some lovely fun memories of Carl from back in the day and whenever I see him there's always a warm hug. He's a class act who's brought joy to dancefloors for years and continues to do so. Big love.'
Nancy Noise

Foreword

BY LAURENT GARNIER

It is a real honour to be writing here about one of the greatest people I have ever met. We all know and love Carl as a king of the dancefloor, and watching him in action is such a joy. But Carl Cox is so much more than just an amazing DJ, he's a truly wonderful person. You couldn't ask for a more thoughtful and caring friend, and our friendship has been there from day one.

I first met Carl in New York in the very early 1990s and I instantly felt like I'd known him for years. We were at the New Music Seminar in New York and, like everyone who meets Carl, I was instantly drawn to his personality. I'd seen him from a distance at some raves in the UK but had never spoken to him. What struck me was his immense passion for the music that I loved and his belief in what we were all trying to do. These were the early days of the scene and none of us knew if it would or could last but Carl was all about the music and, scene or no scene, I could see that would never change. I flew him straight over to the Rex in Paris and could see that he instantly bonded with the crowd without fully understanding how mesmerised we all were watching him play.

No matter how big he's become as a DJ he has remained true to his original pioneering underground spirit. Carl is not like most underground DJs. He can play anything to anyone anywhere and make something special happen. He is the most energetic person I know, and he puts a lot of this energy into his music. When you know Carl's personality it all makes sense; like with everything he does, when he plays he gets straight to the point. His positive and open-minded attitude comes through in the music and it's like he's glowing, with his own visible aura. In fact, glowing is a good way to think of Carl because it's like he's surrounded by an energy force that fills every room he's in and helps light the way forward.

Even when he's concentrating it seems like he's always smiling. His big smile is famous and it makes you smile too. Anyone who can make you smile and make you dance has got to be doing something right! Everybody loves Carl and Carl loves everybody. He doesn't have a dark side, he's always upbeat, even in his hardest times, and that's what makes him so special. His positivity is out of this world.

Carl has proved to everybody that it is possible to really be something if you believe in yourself. When you look at where he came from and how high he climbed so quickly it became an inspiration to many of us and an example to hundreds of thousands of people. Like when Daft Punk influenced a whole generation of French music makers after they seemed to go straight to the top from one day to the next, but Carl did this first. He has shown people that they too can achieve, partly because he makes everything look so simple. He made the scene accessible, always shaking hands with everyone and saying 'hi' or giving out hugs and spreading his happy vibes. We were both playing at a big rave in Scotland where there were about 15,000 people and a massive queue to get in. I was with Carl and as we walked down the side of the line everyone seemed to be calling out his name and trying to shake his hand – he acknowledged them all individually and I remember thinking 'Wow!' I'd never imagined us DJs could be famous.

The first time he played for me in Paris the crowd at the Rex went absolutely mental. He gave them that Carl Cox magic and the whole club rocked. We have gone on to play together all over the world, often on the same line-ups as Richie Hawtin and Jeff Mills, and have made many memories together. The Rex was the place I have my best memory with Carl and the only time I saw him nervous to play. I'd invited him over for the Rex's fifteenth-anniversary weekend and as part of that we decided to do a rave for kids on the Sunday afternoon. The kids were very little, probably aged from four to eight, and Carl was worried about what to play. It was the only time I ever gave him advice – which was, 'Just be yourself.' And he was. The more he banged it, the crazier the kids went, and when he played 'The Bells' by Jeff Mills and Dave Clarke's 'Red' they went absolutely wild. Little kids were rushing over to get a hug from Big Carl as he dropped some serious techno. Those kids are in their twenties now and some have come up to me to tell me that the afternoon with Carl was one of the best experiences of their lives. Mine too!

Carl is the biggest techno DJ ever and has become an icon who transcends the dance music scene. The aura surrounding him is even bigger than he is. People everywhere know his name, even if they haven't heard him play. All this is from his hard work, his limitless energy and because everything he does he shares with the scene. Carl taught me two things: respect each other; and if you believe in what you do you can go all the way.

Kindness, generosity and positivity are three characteristics that sum up Carl for me. In all the years I have had the privilege of knowing him he has never wavered from displaying these qualities. In France we have a word when someone is totally selfless, and that is *bienveillant*. It isn't easy to translate but it roughly means 'kind all the way round'. That is Carl. The loveliest guy you could ever want to meet. Someone committed to sharing the music he loves with everyone. An incredible human being, one who I am proud to call my friend.

Laurent Garnier,
France 2020

Welcome!

When I was a boy, I cut someone's hedge and afterwards went to get paid the one pound we'd agreed. The guy didn't think I'd done a good enough job and refused to pay me. I'd been outside in the cold and rain for the best part of an hour and he'd been watching me through the window. He waited until I'd finished and tidied up before telling me he wasn't happy. I argued with him and his final reply before slamming the door on me was 'Save it for your book, sonny!' Well, here's the book – say hello to karma from me!

I've thought about telling my story for quite a while but the timing never seemed right. I wanted to be able to do it my way rather than it just be a list of dates and gigs with the odd DJ story. I wanted to share some of the behind-the-scenes stuff that people don't normally get to know and, through the stories, show what makes me tick. I wanted everyone to see what Carl Cox is all about.

My working life is a tale of ups and downs. I went from a supermarket shelf-stacker and scaffolder to a budding DJ living out of the back of a car. I made a big decision to provide sound systems to my friends and then, just when it looked like things were going to work out, it seemed like everyone started running clubs that already had sound systems and I was literally out in the cold. The unlicensed rave scene was my saviour and although I spent a lot of time being chased around the countryside I was finally able to express myself through my music. But even then I never imagined that I would go on to become a successful DJ and artist, own a motorsports team, become the most listened-to DJ on the planet, win awards, headline festivals all over the world and that in 2021 I'd be bigger and more popular than ever before.

Dance music is now the soundtrack to everything we do - it is the soundtrack of now and of tomorrow. I can't believe how far I've come and how far I think I can go. Despite all the success, and whether I'm behind the decks or in front of them, I am still very much the same Carl Cox I always was, still driven by my love of music and my desire to share it with everyone, everywhere. I'm one of the crowd and I just love being part of what's going on. I can't see that ever changing - and why would I want it to?

Oh yes, oh yes!

Carl Cox,
Melbourne 2021

1.

Oh No, Oh No!

It's Sunday, 4 November 2007, and I'm on a flight to Barbados to see my parents. They're not expecting me, and I wasn't planning on going there, but my dreams are shattered and I don't know what to do.

I'm running away. I've decided to quit performing, to walk away from the thing I love the most. I need to get away from dance music and be with people who don't see me as a DJ. I need to be with Mum and Dad. Overnight, I've decided to change back from DJ Carl Cox to plain old Carl.

My tour manager, Ian Hussey, is in the next seat to me. He's looking exhausted, and he never looks exhausted. The last twenty-four hours have taken their toll. I've just told him that we need to cancel my South American tour, which is already underway, and he's had to relay this news to my management team so they can hit the phones to the promoters in their various countries first thing Monday. I know everyone is going to try to talk me out of this when I land but it feels like a blanket has been thrown over the fire that music ignites in me. I've grabbed a one-way ticket from Venezuela to Barbados. I'm going under the radar. I just want to escape before the shit hits the fan.

*

Two days earlier my head was in a totally different place. The weekend had started well. I'd arrived in Venezuela ready to take on South America. I'd been there a couple of years before, playing a VIP show in a hotel complex, and loved it. The people, the culture, the vibe, it all suited me perfectly and now I was back to headline a festival and share my sound across a whole continent. It was exciting to be there. I'd met lots of Venezuelans at Space in Ibiza and promised that I would come over.

The promoters wanted to show me the sights, but I was itching to get to the venue where I'd be playing the next day. It was Friday and the festival was already underway when I arrived at Caracas's La Rinconada Terrace, where I was playing as part of the Red Noise Festival. It looked great and they'd done a fantastic job on the sound system - which is always the first thing I look at. I'd heard the stories about Venezuela being a dangerous place but all I could see was crowds of people coming together and dancing. Ian thought the security looked a bit young and inexperienced, 'just kids', but when we brought this up we were told, 'Don't worry, everything is cool,' and I suppose we just went along with it.

Saturday came and, like any big show day, I was starting to focus on the music, thinking about what I might play while getting into the local vibe as I walked around town. Fans were around me all day, thanking me for coming to Caracas, big smiles and totally up for it. I had dinner with a bunch of new friends before hitting the venue. It was all happy faces and laughter. Man, I was having fun. People eat late there and after some grilled chicken we headed over to the club for the main event. By the time I arrived it was heaving. We came in through the back of the venue. There seemed to be a shortage of wristbands but security just waved us all through. That should have been a sign, but at the time I just thought that as an artist I didn't need one. Ian went straight to the stage to double-check the set-up, which was perfect. So far so good.

The party kicked off with fireworks and the local support DJ came straight onto a packed dancefloor. The club kept getting busier and there were about 8,000 people going for it. Every time I came onto the stage to check out the crowd I was met by a big cheer. Once again, techno had crossed cultural divides to bring us all together. I was playing a three-hour set from midnight and after a few more fireworks I was on. The crowd erupted, and I was feeding off their energy, ready to go on a journey together. This was a party crowd, responding to every beat and mix as we got into our groove. Great lighting and smoke added to the atmosphere and the promoters had worked hard to make this a special experience. I could hear a load of firecrackers going off, which is a bit distracting when you're perfecting your mix, and I made a mental note to make sure this didn't happen at the next gig. More firecrackers, and I looked up to see chunks of the crowd fleeing the dancefloor - and then I heard the cheers turning to screams. More firecrackers.

I've seen some crazy things from behind the decks and shared some serious emotions with the dancefloor, but I didn't know what panic and fear looked like until that moment. I was still playing and Ian was signalling to me while talking to the promoters, and then someone from behind me shouted in my ear, 'They're shooting!' I was thinking, *WTF, what do I do? Are they shooting at me, who are they?* and a million other things. All the while I kept playing as the dancefloor emptied out. The DJ in me was overriding common sense. I couldn't just kill it, so I slowly drew down the crossfader, letting the track gently go silent, and in the same movement I dropped down behind the decks.

Without the music the screams became deafening. I popped my head up, saw bodies on the ground and pandemonium, and dropped right back down. The stage manager was screaming at us, 'Venga conmigo! Venga conmigo! Come with me! Come with me! Come!' Next thing I was crawling on my hands and knees, following Ian as we got off the stage. Then we were up and running. We reached a locker room by the backstage toilets and barricaded ourselves in, pulling a security guard in with us.

At this point I didn't know what was happening or if the gunmen were still around and if they were after me. A few minutes later we heard more shots and then silence.

Finally there was a knock on the door, but we weren't opening it for anyone. The promoter shouted through that he was leaving a security guy outside the door and that the police were on their way. We had our car brought round the back and, still not knowing what the hell was going on, decided to make a break for it. Ian always goes above and beyond and somehow convinced the police to escort him back up to the stage to pick up the kit. I was having none of it. I just wanted to get as far away as possible. Then, surrounded by police and security, we made our way into the car and back to the hotel. By now it was nearly 3am and we were starting to find out what had happened.

It turned out a local gang member was a fan and with one of his men and both their wives they came to the club to hear me play. As the story goes, the word got out to a rival gang, who turned up, bypassed the security, sought them out and killed them. With so much security present, I was amazed that something like this could happen - four people shot dead less than fifteen metres in front of me, with another nine people wounded in the crossfire. I could never in my worst nightmares have imagined such an atrocity could happen on a dancefloor. I've seen all manner of things but this was dark.

Then the phones started to ring. News services were beginning to run with the story 'Four killed at Carl Cox event' - and the Chinese whispers meant friends were getting calls saying I'd been killed. To add to the craziness of the situation, the guy on stage filming the gig had captured the whole thing, including the bodies on the dancefloor, me ducking below the decks and the aftermath. People were starting to see it online and I could only imagine how chilling it was to see bodies lying dead on the dancefloor where moments earlier they'd been celebrating life. It's now all over the internet but I still can't bring myself to watch it.

Of course, I was oblivious to this. I just wanted to get the fuck out of Dodge. By the time the press found out where I was staying I was already in the air on the way to Barbados.

Barbados is a magical island. Everyone that goes there, even for a short visit, feels the specialness of the place. By 2007 my parents had long since moved back there from the UK, which was perfect for them. Both very unwell, they were surrounded by friends and family. My mum was especially proud of my achievements. I'd made a success of myself, kept out of trouble (for the most part), put a few quid in my pocket with a bit aside for a rainy day, and they could see how happy my music was making me.

This visit was different. I was different. I'll be talking about my folks later on in the book, but for now you can imagine how painful this trip was. My dad was already so affected by his Alzheimer's that he wouldn't have known what was going on and my mum was very sick too. I didn't realise how short a time she was to have left, and I've always felt some peace in the knowledge that she saw how I turned to her in my darkest moment.

I'll come back to my folks later, because it's important to me that the first time you meet my parents is how I want you to remember them, happy and full of life.

My team and I are a close-knit family and after the shootings we had spoken about the tour and the wider picture. I felt it was time for me to step back. If this was where dance music was going, then maybe hanging up my headphones was a wise move. I wasn't thinking straight after what had happened. I guess looking at it now and seeing how it still affects me I was probably in shock, but I was sure that it was game over. Ian has since told me that when I got on the plane I said I was 200 per cent never going back and when we landed a few hours later I was still 100 per cent sure of that.

Lynn Cosgrave at Safehouse had put together the tour alongside my booking agent Ian Hindmarsh; he'd vetted the venues and promoters and done everything humanly possible to help me bring my sound to South America. He was in the frontline and you might expect that he'd push me to get back on the horse, but he knows me really well and could see that I just needed friends around me and no extra pressure. At this point I still wasn't certain if the shooting had been directed at me or not. We agreed that I'd spend a week thinking about what to do and that the tour wouldn't be cancelled but put on hold. Looking back, I was probably at fifty/fifty by this point. Today we understand a lot more about emotional trauma and how long the recovery process can be but back then seven days seemed like a long time. I hadn't been physically injured and a week seemed like a luxury.

What I do is not a typical job. Music is my passion and sharing it has always been my focus. DJs don't go to work, they go to play, and when something is such a big part of your DNA it is almost impossible to live without it. For sure, this was some other-dimension crazy shit, but I'd worked too hard from a standing start to get to where I was to let a bunch of cold-blooded murderers take that away from me. Pretty soon I felt there was a 90 per cent chance that I was back – in fact, I felt like I hadn't been away at all.

In my hardest times it has always been the music that kept me going and made me happy. I remember making the phone call to Ian. I looked in the mirror as I dialled and said to myself, 'I'm Carl Cox, I'm a DJ, the People's Choice, the Three Deck Wizard, I love music and nothing will stop me from making it!' It was a short conversation. Ian had second-guessed me, spoken to all the promoters and had put extra arrangements in place. It wasn't quite playing behind bullet-proof glass (which had been discussed and dismissed by me) but he'd arranged extra security at all the gigs so I was protected from the airport to the car to the hotel to the gig and back again. Looking back, it seems like overkill, but back then without that I wouldn't have been able to focus on the music. (I found out a couple of years later that Ian had also pre-written the cancellation emails as he wasn't sure which way I was going to go.)

The Caracas gig had done me in mentally and had nearly finished my career. In fact, as yet I haven't been back to Venezuela since the shooting and that's something I need to change. I did a lot of soul-searching during that week in Barbados. Maybe I'd achieved everything possible. Maybe it was a sign or a lucky escape. But quickly I started thinking about new ideas and concepts. When you're on the go all day long and every day you don't have time to take stock. That is what I did in Barbados. Performing, producing, collaborating, remixing, creating – music runs to my very soul. There was only one way for me to go and that is the way I always go – forwards. I came back from the brink super-energised with a plan and a clear vision of the direction I wanted to go in. And people all over the world have loved sharing the energy with me ever since. I still can't quite believe how close I came to calling it a day.

So, it was 'bye-bye' Barbados and 'hello again' South America. I was back, but not my usual self. I felt nervous being there, guilty that I'd run from Venezuela in the first place and worried that something would go down again. Dance music had come a long way from the underground rave scene and I felt responsible, that everyone would look at me as an ambassador of the industry. The first gig was very scary. I kept sneaking a peek from backstage to the capacity crowd and trying to see if I could spot any trouble. *One sign and I'll be off, for sure*, I kept thinking.

I knew the crowd were all aware of what had happened. Maybe shootouts were part of the culture, maybe they weren't ready to let themselves go deep into the music. Lots of maybes. *Don't bottle it, Coxy.* As I stepped up on to the stage I felt very exposed. It was like slow motion, and suddenly it hit me. They were here for me and I was here for them. I stood in front of them and the whole crowd started clapping, louder than the music. They weren't just clapping me, they were clapping the whole scene, and with that I launched myself into one of the best sets I've ever played. I'd tried to act solemn and serious but I could feel my face break into a massive smile as I felt that connection.

Boom! Oh yes, oh yes! I was definitely back!

2.

Here I Am

People always think that I was born in Brighton, but here's something you probably don't know – I'm actually a Northerner. Carl Andrew Cox was born in Oldham, near Manchester, in July 1962, and was only transported down South at the age of six months. So I guess that makes me an honorary Northerner. First stop was Tooting Broadway, which was a bustly kind of place and where I lived until I was four or five, before we moved five miles down the road to Carshalton.

My parents came from Barbados and, like many West Indians of their generation, they came to England to work. My father Henry – or, to give him his full name, Henry Carlisle Cox, known as Carl Snr – worked on the buses; Merton Bus Depot was his second home. My mother, Patricia, was a nurse and midwife at St George's hospital in Tooting. My parents worked really hard to give us a good home. And by us, I mean me and my two younger sisters, Andrea and Pamela. We had some cousins from my mum's side living in Harlow and saw them a lot, but apart from these visits we were the only black family in our area and that came with its own problems. But problems are only problems if you let them become so.

My first memories revolve around music. My parents had come over from the Caribbean determined to make the best of things and, even though I can see now that things can't have been easy for them, they made a happy home. My sisters and myself enjoyed the best soul music as it drifted through the house. Dad's record player was meant to be out of bounds but after hearing the likes of Aretha Franklin, Booker T. and the M.G.'s and Elvis Presley I was always trying to play his records and he'd usually turn a blind eye. I didn't realise at the time how much we had bonded through his music, and I only became aware of this when I played his original records on a special virtual show in 2020. I'll come back to that later.

Mum and Dad had a great collection of soul 45s and I would love choosing the right single for the mood in the house and get excited when a family member started to bop around the lounge. It wasn't long before I was working out what to play and in what order to keep the family dancing. I never imagined that you could get a job playing records but I knew that I loved doing it and I particularly loved the feeling of making the right selection. My folks started me off on the path that has led me to where I am today. With all the crazy things kids get up to, my parents were probably relieved that I was spending any money I had on records and not getting myself into trouble. That's not to say that there weren't times when I pushed the envelope a bit too far.

Even from a young age I loved bikes and when I was seven or eight I had a Golden Arrow bicycle, which I was really proud of. One day, I rode off and ended up cycling from Carshalton all the way to Croydon before the police stopped me, realised I was a long way from home and drove me back in their Panda car. My mum looked shocked when the police knocked on the door and saw me sitting in the back, smiling away. My sisters were very jealous that I'd been in a police car.

Luckily my dad was at work at the time, although he might have seen the funny side.

We did cause a major parental explosion another time, when Pamela was cooking sausages for our tea when she was fourteen. She'd left them under the grill and forgotten about them. I was up in my room when I heard a shriek and ran down. The oil had caught fire and the kitchen was filled with black smoke, so I grabbed the pan and carried it out to the front garden, amazingly without getting any of the boiling oil on my legs – although I did slosh it all over the brand-new carpet. By the time my parents came back from work, Andrea and Pamela had run off and hidden, and my folks came into a smoke-filled house, burnt and blackened wallpaper and a stained carpet. All three of us caught it big time.

My mum, God rest her soul, was a great cook and our house always had that homely smell of West Indian cooking. She made a good chicken, rice and peas, but my favourite was the macaroni pie done in the true West Indian style using sweet potato. I think that the food helped them stay connected to the friends and family they had left behind.

My parents really wanted me to focus at school but try as I might, studying really wasn't for me. I did enjoy going to school but as I got older it seemed a big part of the day to be away from the music I loved, so I did the obvious thing. Actually, the obvious thing would have been to cut school, so I ended up doing the second most obvious thing – I took the music to the school. I had a small turntable with a built-in amp and would spend breaktime and lunchtime spinning a few tunes. These were mostly my dad's records, so lots of soul. The other kids seemed to enjoy it and I would watch and see which tunes had the best reactions and mentally file them away as guaranteed floor fillers. By the age of ten I was a full-on vinyl junkie and was spending every bit of my pocket money on funk and soul records. The great thing about living in Carshalton was that people seemed happy to dump their records at the local charity shop and you could pick up some great calypso, soul and jazz if you knew where to look.

Racism played a big part in my school experience. Kids can be cruel, even if they don't mean to be. But some of these kids really *did* mean to be cruel. I tried not to let it bother me but I did think how unfair it was. Being black has never defined me; most of my friends, like me, don't see colour or religion but the person. The bullies soon left me alone, not because I grew to be bigger than all of them, but because I genuinely wasn't bothered.

Karma has a funny way of surfacing when you least expect her to. I remember being in a club and coming down at about 3am for some air. There was still a massive queue outside. I was pretty well known by now and people in the queue would reach out to shake my hand. There was a group of guys and girls shivering outside, waiting their turn and one guy called me over: 'Carl, Carl.' I recognised him as someone who'd given me grief many years before. I walked over, a big smile on my face as usual; he looked at me and said, 'We were at school together.' I looked back at him and said, 'Good for you, mate,' and walked off. Funnily enough, even though all his mates got into the club, for some reason the doormen kept turning him away.

My favourite record as a kid was 'Metal Guru' by Marc Bolan and T. Rex. I didn't know what the lyrics meant, but I loved the music and the energy. It didn't really fit with the music we had at home, but by this point my musical tastes were expanding. Whenever I drive across that little humpback bridge on Gipsy Lane in Barnes I think of Bolan, who died there when the Mini he was being driven in by his girlfriend, Gloria Jones, crashed. I sometimes play Gloria's Northern Soul classic 'Tainted Love' as a tribute to him.

Home wasn't the only place I was hearing stuff. Obviously there was the radio and occasionally television but, being a big lad, I was able to get into clubs from a very early age. By fourteen, I was a full-on clubber. This is where I was hearing new sounds, including records from the USA, and getting down on the dancefloor to twelve-inch versions of the songs I liked. The DJs in the clubs would talk over the records as they introduced them, which I found annoying, but this was the way it was so you just got on and danced.

I like to use a mic when I play, especially now when I might be playing to thousands of people, as it enables me to get even closer to everyone, but from the first time I hit the decks in a club as a 'proper' DJ I have always concentrated on letting my music do the talking for me. The trick to using a mic is knowing when *not* to use it. Of course, going clubbing and buying records was not cheap and I was holding down lots of jobs at the same time to be able to pay for everything.

Anyone into vinyl will tell you how special it used to feel to find a tune that you were after. You'd always have your eyes open and you'd be popping into every charity shop near you at least once a week to see if anything cool had landed. I was doing lots of odd jobs to make cash to buy more records and had the bright idea of buying records cheaply to sell on to my mates at a profit. Of course, anyone who collects records will tell you that this was going to end in disaster. The saying 'Don't get high on your own supply' was probably invented for vinyl junkies. I don't think I ever sold on one record, I just couldn't part with them. Somewhere among my over 150,000 pieces of vinyl will be a couple of Barry White singles with 'Property of Carl' scrawled on the cover. I remember telling Terry Farley about them once in the early acid house days when he used to regularly play Barry's 'It's Ecstasy When You Lay Down Next To Me'. In those days any track that had the word 'Ecstasy' in it was played over and over.

From a very young age, I'd been building up my cash stockpile. It was mostly in coins and fitted in a tin under my bed, but every coin was earned with sweat. Before I would go to school, I would do a milk round and, several times a week, I would also do a paper round. I would then earn a few quid cutting people's grass and trimming privets. I was like a handyman, except that I was only a child. In the little spare time I had, I was putting together my own sound system. I thought I really knew what I was doing and that I was being really clever putting it together from discarded speakers and amps. I'd already been playing my records for my mates and now the big day was arriving. I had my first gig! It was a school disco but this was special, as lots of different schools were coming together. I was fourteen and ready to rock the party. I'd been thinking about DJ names, but couldn't work out something that I liked, so I thought I'd just stick with DJ Carl Cox. I could always think of another name later.

Anyway, here I was, ready to be the king of the school disco, the envy of all the boys and the hero to all the girls. What could go wrong? Well, the main thing that could go wrong was that I could screw it up, and boy, did I screw this one up. When I got to the hall, I realised my rig was just not big enough. I spread the speakers around the room as best I could and used every bit of tape I could find to stick the wires to the floor, so that people wouldn't trip over them. I had all my records ready and now my years of hard work, earning that money to buy all that stuff and put it all together, was about to reap dividends. I played my music loud at disco level and it wasn't long before the system couldn't take it. One by one, the speakers and amplifiers started to blow. It started off with the tweeters, moving on to the mid cones, before the bass finally packed in as well. Party done. People had actually had a good time. For most of us, it was a chance to hang out with girls and wear our best gear. I put on a brave face, but only I knew how disappointed I was. That's when I realised I needed a proper system.

Just like when, years later, I would run to Barbados from Venezuela, I knew who I could turn to for help. Mum. I didn't need moral support this time – what I needed was a new sound system. Now my mum, like most mums, I guess, bought stuff out of catalogues. The Freemans catalogue had a disco system that cost a whopping £570 (equal to about £3,000 today). I was fifteen and £570 might as well have been £5 million. I don't think the people of Carshalton could drink enough milk or read enough newspapers for me to make that kind of money quickly. However, the beauty of the catalogue system is that you can pay it off on a weekly basis and, for the princely sum of £2.50 per week, this magnificent disco set with amplifier, speakers, lights and turntables could be mine. This was basically an entry-level sound system, but to me it was like hitting the jackpot. My mum agreed to put it in her name and guarantee the payment and I would pay her back £2.50 per week. She had never told me how much she believed in me but this act told me everything I needed to know. Now that I had a proper system, I was able to get out there as a real mobile DJ, offering my disco services to weddings, bar mitzvahs, schools, scout troops, pubs and anyone who'd have me.

I still had all my side 'businesses' on the go. I was also a decorator and could turn my hand to most things. Like all young decorators, you start off as a knotter. Knotting is taking the knots out of skirting boards and you do that by treating every knot. A lorry load turns up with row after row of skirting boards on it, you take each one off, dab each knot with a grey primer, then you rub it down. Then you put two undercoats on it and let it dry. After that, you gloss over it – and yes, it is as boring as it sounds. And by boring, I mean backbreakingly, mind-numbingly boring. I did this solidly for a year and a half. I don't think the people employing me knew I was only fifteen, although they paid me as if I was.

My turning sixteen was like the school bell sounding at the end of the day – it was time to go. I left school as soon as I could, ready to make my way in the world, and never looked back. I'd been working at all sorts of pocket-money jobs since I was eight, so being free of school gave me all the hours in the day to graft. This record collection was going to grow, oh yes!

Selling records was a bust so I needed a new plan, and at sixteen your avenues are slightly limited. I was already taking a bag of records to parties and friends' houses, not because they were asking me but because I wanted to. So I decided to get into the mobile disco business. I got my first pair of decks with a small system. The decks were belt-driven rather than direct-drive like the amazing Technics 1200s, so there was a lot of blending and fading to try and work out how to get the music to work. Twelve-inch records would give the dancefloor more time to get into it but they were much more expensive than seven-inch singles, more than double. I hit on the idea of buying two of the same seven-inches because many of them had instrumentals on the B side and so, with a bit of practice and experimenting, I could keep the groove going – not that it saved me much money though.

I started to play as many parties as I could and feeling the buzz from the crowd made the effort so worthwhile. At sixteen the only way I could be truly mobile was if I got a lift, and there was the odd time when I'd be lugging everything on a bus, doing several trips while I was setting up.

I was mainly playing soul, disco, funk and early hip-hop with a little bit of electro thrown in. Even then I was looking for the perfect combination of sounds for me. I loved the energy of a live band – it doesn't get much better than the raw funk workouts on the JB's recordings where you can hear the likes of Clyde Stubblefield, Maceo Parker, Fred Wesley and Bootsy Collins under the direction of the Godfather himself, James Brown. But then I also felt the beauty in the rhythms created by computerised drum machines by the likes of Giorgio Moroder and Gary Numan. What I needed to do, although I hadn't quite worked this out at the time, was to mix the two. I needed to combine the layered beats and rhythms that were machine made but designed by humans with the soulful vocals that can only be manmade.

Aside from my fledgling mobile disco business, by the age of sixteen I was also a shelf-stacker at the local supermarket and was cutting the grass for Sutton Council. Even though I hadn't done well at school, I've never been lazy. Working hard, no matter how mundane or boring the job, was something that I'd learned from my parents. And it was this quality that set me up for the future. Of course, I couldn't know at the time just how far working hard and putting the hours in would get me.

Funnily enough, cutting the grass for Sutton Council was a great gig for me. It got me out in all weathers as I went around Carshalton and I received the handsome sum of £71 per week. It also kept me fit and meant that I had more money to spend on going out and buying records. I remember one time when I was cutting the grass on a roundabout and the 157 bus came past. As I looked up, I saw all my friends on that bus, laughing and pointing at me. They hadn't known I was doing this job and when I saw them later that night, they had a good laugh at my expense. I still know some of these guys today and whenever we get together, this story always pops up.

Sometimes, people would shout racist comments at me as I was cutting the grass. I would wonder what was going through their minds. They'd be driving along and see a black guy sweating away cutting the grass to make their town look great for them and they'd go to all the trouble of winding down the window to shout something at him that they thought would make him feel bad. Was that designed to make me cut the grass worse or better? Was it done to make them feel better about themselves? Did they feel better later on or did they suddenly realise what they had done could be hurtful to me? In fact, I don't suppose any of this would go through their minds at all. Some people are just plain old ignorant and the thing about ignorant people is, it's nothing to do with me – it's their problem.

Surprisingly, I then thought I'd give education another go. I was still sixteen, so I thought maybe now I was ready to do something I really liked. I enrolled at Carshalton College and, including the two and a half months of holidays, I spent six months studying motor mechanics and electrical engineering. Unfortunately, the course was supposed to last three years and I'm not sure that the two and a half years that I wasn't there would have been exciting enough to compensate for the boredom I experienced in those first six months. This proved to me once and for all that study was not for me. I like working with my hands and every hour I was sitting in that college, I wasn't out there earning – and I knew that I needed to earn all the time. My parents had already been talking about moving back to Barbados and I knew that I might suddenly have to pay my way – and I didn't want to give up on my music and my dreams.

What I did learn at college, funnily enough, in those six months, would be something that I still use to this day. I learned how to make my own speaker system and I also learned how to strip down and rebuild a car engine. I could have stuck out this course and might have done, not just to make my parents happy but because I actually enjoyed the practical side of what I was learning. The bottom line is, I wanted to earn cash. The more I went out, the more I could see what I didn't have. I'm not a greedy person, but who doesn't want to look good and have the same kind of fun that all your friends are having?

So, at this point, I was a shelf-stacker, a grass-cutter, a painter and decorator, a mobile DJ, a general handyman and an odd-job man who also delivered milk and newspapers. I had lots of jobs but no career and no prospect of one on the horizon. To me a career just seemed to mean a job that you did for many years. I'd find out later that a career was something you built; I couldn't imagine ever saying that I had one myself. Little did I know how soon this was all going to change.

3.

Do the Hustle

Most of my jobs were just about making money. But the disco business was different. I was born to play music. I even managed to get a loan from the Prince's Trust which helped me get going. I spent it on sound equipment, so thank you very much HRH for giving me a chance.

The biggest dancefloor filler from my mobile disco days was Lulu's version of the Isley Brothers track 'Shout'. It had been a hit for her in 1964 but was still going strong in the 1980s and was the 'Jump Around' of my day. From the minute that voice warbles out the word 'Well' and the hairs on the back of your neck have stood up, you know what's coming next. Little Lulu says the words: 'You know you make me want to . . .' and at that point, the crowd goes mad. No other record is like that. People would go into a frenzy as they got more and more into it. The kind of places I was playing like pubs and social clubs, it was almost guaranteed that a fight would break out during the song. It was a bit like a mosh pit today, people were just ramming into each other, with one last burst of craziness before they went back to their daily lives.

Most of my music was funk, soul and disco, and I'd only play the odd pop song if I really liked it. I didn't take many requests, but that was mainly because the stuff they were asking for, I didn't have. Today, you can walk around with a couple of USB sticks in your pocket containing thousands of tracks, but the craft of the DJ was built around vinyl. I'm not a purist when it comes to vinyl - though I do love it and prefer it - because I can create so much more with the new digital systems, meaning I'm less inclined to do my vinyl sets. But the reason that vinyl was so important is it wasn't just about *how* you played, but about *what* you played. A record box is heavy. Two record boxes are twice as heavy. Two record boxes and a bag over your shoulder is twice as heavy again, so what you played became as important as how you played it because you had to take everything with you. If you weren't able to judge the crowd and their mood, you could end up playing your floor fillers too early and then either running out of music or repeating what they'd already heard. At the same time - and this applies to vinyl or CD/digital - just because you like something doesn't mean that everybody else will like it so you have to get the balance between playing stuff that people are familiar with and stuff that you want them to hear. Norman Jay does this very well and can drop the most obscure funk B-side before bringing it back with a big floor-filling anthem.

Things were going well and I was saving a bit of money so I thought I'd treat myself to my first foreign holiday. I remember booking it through a company called 'Nat's Coaching Holidays' and I boarded a coach that would eventually take me to Cap d'Agde, a seaside resort on France's Mediterranean coast. After I booked the trip and told my mates where I was going, one of them said to me: 'Isn't that where they have the naturist beaches?' I was very pleased that the beaches that I was heading for were full of nature. I imagined that it would mean unspoilt, sandy beaches. By the time I got to France, though, I had found out what a naturist beach meant and knew there was no damn way that I'd be getting my tackle out for all to see.

A friend of mine, who I could probably say was my first girlfriend (although I must say that we were really more friends than anything else), was going to come with me and we packed our bags, excited to head off to the campsite. I was seventeen and looking forward to a bit of freedom. The thing about freedom, though, is you sort of need the experience of life to go with it, and back home my general welfare was always taken care of by my mum and sisters. The first night in France I was introduced to sangria and got absolutely hammered. I think one of the reasons I got so drunk was that I was nervous, because I thought this would be the night that our kissing might go further.

The next day, we hit the beaches and had a really good time, although I had a very sore head. That night, I had a plan. We were drinking away now that we were sangria experts, and when I got to the point where I was absolutely about to go over the edge, we stopped drinking to go to the all-you-can-eat barbecue. I love barbecue food, and it tastes even greater when you're drunk. As I said, it was all-you-can-eat, and I didn't want the French to think I was being rude so I really went to town on that barbecue. When I was fit to burst, we moved back on to sangria and kept drinking. Now, I thought, was the perfect time to move in for a kiss. I moved forward seductively, at which point I threw up violently everywhere. On everything and everyone. Amazingly, none of it went on me and I felt a lot better. Funnily enough, we didn't really get it together on that trip but we had a smashing time and came back as great friends. I vowed never to drink sangria again - and one day soon I will start to implement that vow.

Things were going well. It was 1980, a new decade, and I was getting ready to become a fully fledged man and turn eighteen. Would I have a party? Would I DJ at my own party? I knew a lot of great venues, ranging from pubs and clubs to warehouse spaces. So it seems an odd choice that I would spend my eighteenth in HM Prison Blantyre House, a category C/D resettlement prison and detention centre in Kent. Of course, it wasn't *my* choice. I was sent there at the age of seventeen, having been given a three-month sentence and knowing that I was very lucky – if I had been eighteen, I could have ended up in a much more serious place and that could have sent me on a downward spiral. I didn't do anything that was too naughty and it didn't harm anyone, but the consequences could have been tragic. I haven't talked about this before so it makes sense to explain what happened here.

I had been driving from about the age of sixteen, obviously with no licence, and I loved to drive fast. I still do, but now I have a licence and, with the responsibilities of owning a racing team, understand about safety. At sixteen, I just wanted to go fast and was picking up very cheap cars to do it in. I was what you would call a multiple offender: speeding, street racing, all that kind of stuff. In fact, by the time I was sixteen, even though I didn't have a driving licence, I had ten points against any driving licence I might get in the future. It wasn't long before I picked up a few more points and lost the possibility of getting a licence when I turned seventeen. This basically meant that if I passed a driving test I would be banned from driving as soon as I qualified for the licence.

Now, I was pulled over a lot. Not really because I was black, but because I just couldn't seem to slow down. And once I was pulled over, it would come out that I had no licence, and hence no insurance – I must confess I didn't bother with MOTs too much either. Being the only black family in the area, the local police knew the family well. My parents were well liked and well respected and I didn't really want the police to keep knocking on my door and tell my parents what I was getting up to. I decided to only drive cars the police didn't know I was connected to, which normally meant friends' cars. The crucial day I was stopped, I was driving my good mate's car. I had been tempted to floor it but, luckily, I didn't. If I had done, my life could have been very different. I was given another driving ban, so now I was doubly banned, although I still didn't have a licence to endorse, and was also sentenced to three months inside. I think they were trying to send a message and make a point to the other boy racers. Whatever the motive, going into prison was a crushing blow. Worse than that was the disappointment I knew my parents must have felt. It wasn't where I'd ever thought I'd end up because, apart from the driving, I'd gone out of my way to stay out of trouble.

My eighteenth birthday was very lonely. I didn't feel like I'd become a man, but it did make me realise what an idiot I had been. I knew that I could turn things around and do things properly. I would see out the bans and make sure that I drove safely – and legally – in the future. Being a mobile disco and not having any wheels makes you slightly less mobile than you'd like to be. But I stuck to my guns and made it work.

I've always liked cars and bikes. I'd had a nice little 50cc Yamaha to get around on and when I was driving with no licence, I wasn't pulled up for ages. After my big run-in with the law, I went on to pass my driving test at eighteen and, once I'd paid off all the fines, my points went back to zero. I made sure never to lose my licence again.

Anyway, when I came out of prison I was eighteen and still living with my parents, which does sort of cramp your style. I had a great crew around me, guys and girls, that would all hang out together and go out dancing. In fact, other than my short stay at Her Majesty's pleasure, I was probably out almost every weekend from the age of sixteen to eighteen. One of the girls in our crew would be my first! I really fancied her, but I don't think she fancied me at all at the beginning. The more time we spent together, though, the more I felt she really liked me; in the end, she saw something in me that was different to the other guys around us and felt that I was a decent guy to be with. I remember taking her to a Chinese restaurant in Wimbledon, I think it was called 'Mrs May's', and feeling very grown-up as an eighteen-year-old sitting at a fancy restaurant on a date. She lived around the corner from us and, with my mum, dad and sisters asleep upstairs, and a mixture of fear and excitement, in the dark in our front room we became each other's first love. It was amazing – and probably even more amazing that no one came down considering all the noise we were making. Not that we'd have noticed them if they had come down. I was like a greyhound out of the traps. We were on each other at every opportunity and we both knew that this wasn't going to be forever, but we had the best time. When it did end, it ended on a happy note, and even now I think of her very fondly.

My mate Jim had a scaffolding business. He was also part of a bigger scaffolding company that organised hospitality tents at places like the Farnborough Airshow and the Chelsea Flower Show. If you ever saw a blue and white marquee at any of these shows in the mid-80s, chances are that it was me that helped put it up. In between the big jobs, Jim would bring me on domestic jobs, like scaffolding for window cleaning and roof repairs. The firm also worked for the police, putting up scaffolding and screens around crime scenes. Jim would often bring me along to help him put these up quickly so the police could go in and do what they needed to.

Jim and I are still very close and work together when we can. His expertise is building level dancefloors for outdoor events and what I learned with him there means that wherever I go to play at a new festival, the first thing I do is make sure that the production team have got the flooring right. Jim's recently come on board to do the build for Carl Cox Motorsport at the London Motor Show.

I was part of a great crew. We saw ourselves as fun-loving soul heads. We were really into funk, soul and rare groove but enjoyed a bit of heavy rock and reggae too. We prided ourselves on being all about the music; we were peace-loving but we did watch each other's backs and were always ready to defend ourselves if anyone had a go at us. The funk and soul clubs were great and our crew, which was a mixture of male and female and black and white, would fit right in. Black and white didn't really mix in the mainstream world, though, and in the commercial clubs you would definitely see a fight or two. We'd be watching each other's backs and it would be a good night for us if there was no fight at all or a bad night if there was a fight that didn't sort itself out quickly. There were also terrible nights where the fighting seemed to go on and on and people ended up in hospital. Fortunately, my size put most people off from picking a fight with me - and in any case, I am much too pretty to end up in hospital!

Most people don't realise what the role of the bouncers in the nightclubs is. The bouncers back then didn't have to be licensed or have any sort of training, they just needed to be big, strong and scary. What people don't understand is that the bouncers were not there to protect the people. The bouncers were there to protect the nightclub. That is why when a fight kicked off the bouncers didn't try and contain it, they moved everyone out on the pavement to fight outside. That way, the club and the furniture don't get smashed up, the punters in the club can keep on buying drinks and the police can deal with the mess outside. To be fair, there would have been little they could do because if you imagine that each crew fighting was maybe twenty people strong and two or three crews could be going at it, there was very little that four bouncers could do about it. Today things are different. Bouncers have turned into doormen, doormen have turned into security and security are well trained, fully licensed, regulated and often have first-aid training too.

We were really into the whole underground rare groove scene and already some DJs were making a name for themselves. I was following Trevor Fung and tried to go to every party he was at. More than any other DJ, he understood the dancefloor and I learned by watching him and watching the crowd and watching my feet moving that understanding the dancefloor was the key to being a great DJ. Up until this point, I would say I was a decent DJ. I played good tunes in the right order and played with passion. Watching Trevor and the ease with which he controlled that dancefloor helped me realise what it would take to be a great DJ.

You meet a lot of people when you're clubbing and it didn't take long for people to know that I had a good record collection and a passion for playing. Ray Lock was an established DJ playing at clubs across London and he would let me warm up for him. I can remember the first time I played for him and the pride I felt walking through the door carrying my record boxes and the doorman just waving me through.

The years that I had put in playing on belt-drive record players balanced on wonky tables, perfecting my skills under those difficult conditions, meant that when I was let loose in clubs that had state-of-the-art direct-drive turntables, proper mixers with crossfaders, and powerful sound systems, I delivered the goods. I spent a lot of time listening to Trevor and it was here that I started to meet his mates like Paul Oakenfold and Trevor's cousin, Ian St Paul. They liked me coming to their parties because I would travel up with a crew of about thirty or forty people ready to dance.

There is a big dance music community down on the South Coast and there's always someone to hang out and have fun with. I remember about a decade later, in the 1990s when I had 'made it', having a chat about music with Fatboy Slim at his place while we were playing table football. I got so carried away that I wrenched the whole stick out and ended up waving my three little plastic players away in the air. He hasn't invited me back to play since, even though he knows that I know he has another table!

Playing table football with megastars was not even a pipe dream for the teenage me. I was really getting into the whole London clubbing thing when my parents threw a bit of a curve ball my way. They had decided that they wanted to move back to Barbados and, at the same time, me and my sisters were going to relocate to Brighton, where I felt I could get more regular paid work. We spoke to the council and they found a property that we could rent from them. I lived there with my sisters after my parents moved back, before I would eventually move out to my own place. One of the jobs I took to make ends meet was as a carpet cleaner. I mean, how hard could it be? I'd work in the middle of the night and it was mostly cleaning the clubs and bars in and around Brighton. This wasn't fun at all and I didn't stick at it for long, but I did meet lots of club owners who would go on to book me later on.

In Brighton, I'd start off by playing in little jazz bars where they'd only pay me if the place got busy. Sometimes it did and sometimes it didn't. It was the same situation at the various shebeens and drinking holes where I could blag myself into. I was also playing in warehouses, where I'd bring my sound system and charge a pound to get in. Having a sound system meant I was always on and it wasn't unusual to get in at 4am and get a knock on the door from friends looking for the next place to go on to before ending up on the beach throwing a free party.

I was still clubbing in London and it was at this point that I started to become really friendly with the key DJs and promoters who would go on to launch the acid house scene a couple of years later. My parties were going from strength to strength and at the end of 1987 when Oakenfold opened his Project club it was me who provided the sound system. I was already making a name for myself as a good, solid warm-up DJ in the West End. In a sense, you could say it was a little bit of a step back to suddenly be providing sound systems for other DJs, but I could see that the scene was going to grow and that everyone who was part of it in any shape or form would be swept along for the ride.

There's a lot of ego attached to the music business and I also wanted my share of success. But coming from where I did, I think I saw success in a slightly different way to some of the others. Some of them were already working in the music biz while I was cleaning carpets. I felt that I had already achieved a lot musically and I could see that everything I was doing was like some sort of apprenticeship where I was learning little bits from a lot of people. Those little nuggets, when stuck together, would make one big piece of gold and, even at that age, I could see that if I had enough experience when I made my move, I would have the potential to overtake everyone else.

Somehow, I think I knew that the 1990s was going to be my big moment. I loved what I was doing and while I had been working to live, now I was living to work. I just wanted more and more. So here I was, at the beginning of 1988, warming up at the Project as dance music and the whole culture around it began to take off. Acid house was coming to the masses, and I was ready and waiting.

4.

One Foot in the Rave

Being a guy with a sound system has a lot of disadvantages. All your mates want to use it for free, you have to drive it around and store it, and you have to get gigs to make it pay for itself. That was the hardest part: weddings, bar mitzvahs, pub discos – I was all over them. It does, however, have one big advantage – and that is you have your own sound system!

My sound system was known to lots of promoters, especially as I was selling tickets for their events and bringing party goers up from Brighton and Hove to some of the London parties. Some of the best-known sound systems were used by their own crew at their own events. The Soul II Soul system came with Jazzie B, Aitch Bee, Daddae, Jazzi Q and all the other Funki Dredds, as we were introduced to 'A happy face, a thumpin' bass, for a lovin' race!' My system was mainly for hire and was known for its sound quality.

My sound system was in demand – all the DJs on the scene wanted to book me. It wasn't just because I had great amps and speakers but because I had something unique, which everyone wanted. And no, that wasn't me. It was a console. A console is basically a flight case mixed with a table that allows you to have all your system, decks and mixer at the perfect position to play from and be sturdy so that the records don't jump. My console was not any old thing. Even in those early days it was a piece of dance music heritage. The console you got when you booked Carl Cox's sound system was none other than the one that legendary DJ Froggy had installed at the Sheffield Arms, which was a pub outside East Grinstead where people went to party. When the Sheffield Arms closed down, I bought the console, which was a bit like a giant coffin. This allowed me to be mobile at any club and rave party.

Froggy really understood sound and I remember hearing him playing 'Space Princess' by Lonnie Liston Smith on a quadrophonic sound system - it just made me tingle all over. Quadrophonic meant that the sound was all around you and by manipulating the treble and the bass, he could literally blow your mind. Froggy was the man for me and one of the most influential people in my early career. Now, because I had this console, I ended up with all the DJs of the day playing on it. Everyone from Pete Tong to Bob Jones were using my system and I got to meet everyone and watch what they played and how they played it.

Having my own sound system meant I could make sure that I could deliver the music in the best way possible. I've played on some terrible rigs in my time and it wasn't long before the party flyers would also talk about the amount of turbo sound, laser and lighting you were getting. The kit quickly became as important as the DJs playing on it. I remember one time when the DJ before me - and he's a friend, so I can't name names - was getting distortion and feedback. He was signalling to the engineer, who was ignoring him, and when he finally caught his eye the sound guy just laughed. That was it, he jumped down and gave him a good pasting. That sorted things out pretty quickly and the sound guy's assistant, now promoted to head man, had things running smoothly in no time.

I'd met many of the up-and-coming DJs, and the promoters who were also DJs, like Nicky Holloway, appreciated the effort I put in to getting the sound right. Nicky's Special Branch Events would bring some of the characters together who would go on to be a big part of the dance scene. Danny Rampling was kind of like Nicky's apprentice and in the summer of 1987 they went to Ibiza on a lads' holiday with Johnny Walker to celebrate Paul Oakenfold's birthday. Out there they met up with Trevor Fung, who was already an established DJ, and Nancy Turner, who would go on to become Nancy Noise. It was Trevor and Nancy who took them to Amnesia on that fateful night where they experienced Alfredo playing under the stars. They had their awakening there and came back as the Ibiza Four. People often ask me why I didn't go with them and the answer is simple - I was invited but I couldn't afford it!

When they came back they wanted to share the Amnesia experience and were sure that people were ready for it. Maybe they were, but the venues weren't interested. So they decided to organise it themselves.

Oakey, being Oakey, was first off the mark. He's always really motivated and knows what he wants. He got hold of this venue in Streatham on Friday nights and would turf everyone out at 2am, reopening as the Project Club and only letting in people who understood the music he'd experienced in Ibiza. Of course, he needed a sound system, and so he came to me. The thing was, I didn't own any decent turntables, I always hired them as needed, but that didn't stop Paul. He wanted to make sure that I always had a pair on hand. Ever the businessman, Paul bought me the turntables then hired them back from me alongside my sound system, and from what he paid me I'd pay him off for the turntables. They were so expensive that I could never have afforded a pair – I think they were about £1,500 and my car only cost ninety quid. Even now, whenever I see him he reminds me that I'm still one or two payments short.

Most clubbers have a ritual when they get ready to go out. Getting ready to go clubbing is the start of an adventure. For me, heading up to the Project to set up my sound system and play a few records was more of an ordeal. Starting out in Brighton, where I was living, I would get the train to East Croydon and then change there for Norbury while carrying two record boxes and a shoulder bag. I would then head over to a mate's place, which was close to Streatham, so I could pick up the sound system and get it to the Project. I'd then be setting up the sound system, playing, dancing until the very end, and then packing everything up and getting the kit back to my mate's place before getting back on the train and doing the whole journey in reverse back to Brighton, while still carrying all the records. I must have really loved what I was doing.

The main reason I was there was for my sound system, but I'd also play at the Project. It was so exciting and fresh. Pre-1987, it was all about rare groove and hip-hop. You would get some house music at certain London clubs but normally only where the cool crowd were, and I wasn't in that crowd. Suddenly, with the whole Balearic thing and the mixing of styles and crowds, it wasn't about a particular style but about great records. There was also fantastic stuff coming out of the States and I was hearing it being played in a special way at this after-hours club and I was at the heart of what was going on.

One night Paul brought the legendary Alfredo over. They actually booked Alfredo to come and play from Amnesia in Ibiza. He travelled hundreds of miles to be there from the land of the sun and he played with his shirt open. He came in with this aura about him, he knew that these people who'd booked him had been to his club in Ibiza, danced outside under the stars, enjoying his music, enjoying the moment. Bringing that whole vibe to south London at that time was unheard of. I knew I was witnessing something special. I was all about the music and suddenly I was in a room full of people just as into it as I was. It was like watching the future unfold in front of your eyes.

Unfortunately, although we probably all guessed it, Paul hadn't mentioned that this club night that was being held in a restaurant was unlicensed and that the restaurant manager was just letting us have the place on the sly. So, kicking off at 2am and going all the way through so that the sweaty clubbers spilling out into the morning sunlight were mixing with people going about their daily business couldn't last forever. The night that Alfredo played was the night we were closed down. There was a supermarket around the corner and one of the clubbers had parked over their loading bay, which meant that none of the vans could deliver the produce, so the police were called to move the car. I suspect that hearing thumping beats at 8am coming from a supposedly closed restaurant filled with hundreds of people may have caught their eye.

The Project was over, but in a sense 'the project' had only just begun.

Next stop for me was Shoom. Of all the Ibiza Four, Danny Rampling was the most affected by what he had seen and heard. He'd been looking for some direction in his life and found it within Alfredo's sound. I'd been playing in Kingston when Danny first approached me. I was playing early house and garage and was really concentrating on finding as much new music as possible. I was beginning to have the tunes I wanted to play for a crowd that would be into it so that I could move things forward musically. Danny was talking about setting up his own club based on his newfound influences and it sounded like the place for me. I could see that Danny was thinking he'd get my sound system and me as a sort of bargain double deal, but I didn't mind – with his ideas it felt like an honour to play there. He'd taken over a fitness centre in Southwark and, with his soon-to-be wife Jenni on the door, he prepared to launch Shoom.

There wasn't much in the way of production – a couple of banners and the smoke machines – but this little box room became the launching pad for acid house, with Danny as the first superstar DJ. For a new scene it was important to have someone with his vision. Obviously, our career paths went in different ways, but we were trying to fight the same cause. Danny was always a great programmer; at that time it was infectious, I really loved to see how he rose above where DJing was supposed to stop. He made a Balearic sound and style for himself, knowing it was something that he owned and no one else. He had the smiley face logo, the Danny dance and the belief that this was his mission.

The opening night of Shoom arrived with my sound system in place and me as the warm-up. Not a lot of people know this, but I actually gave Danny beat mixing lessons before we opened. Before house it was all about funk, soul, rare groove and hip-hop. Suddenly the heartbeat of the dancefloor jumped from 98 beats per minute to 120/122 BPM.

Anyway, we put the decks up, I stuck a piece of A4 paper saying 'Carl Cox' on the wall behind them, opened the doors and away we went. I remember going outside to see this massive queue with half of these people dressed in funky clothes with big platform shoes and thinking, *You guys have no idea what you are in for, cos for sure there is no rare groove tonight.* I think Danny wanted to have some support from me. He knew I could play and that I had the sounds. Everyone came to dance and sweat, people just had a really good time. We knew there was something good going on and that this was just the beginning. It was out with rare groove and in with house music and Balearic beats.

This sounds like a bit of a cliché but the music really did transform everybody. Anything was possible. It was like if you weren't into it there was something wrong with you, as if you didn't understand it. Everyone came together and the scene was ready to explode. You'd have trendy shop girls from Vivienne Westwood dancing alongside proper football fans from Tottenham Hotspur who in turn would be hugging diehard Chelsea fans. Among the crowd were future Shoom residents like Andrew Weatherall, Terry Farley and Pete Heller, and the Boy's Own posse who created the fanzine that documented the scene and would then go on to sign bands like the Chemical Brothers and Underworld. Finally, I was part of something big.

Except I wasn't.

A couple of weeks later Danny and Jenni let me go for no apparent reason. They brought in Joey and Norman Jay's Good Times sound system and replaced me on the decks too. That really hurt. I could see how much the crowd had responded to my music and how much I still had to give. At the same time, Paul wound the Project down as he prepared to open up at Heaven with Spectrum and his Theatre of Madness. He didn't need a sound system there as the club already had one, and it didn't occur to him that I wanted to be much more than just a sound guy. We'd go on to work together many times over the years but for now I was out on my ear.

This was a real low point and in hindsight I should have spoken to Paul about it there and then, but pride gets in the way. Paul was already developing a pop star aura around himself and suddenly I felt very distant and that I was missing the boat again. I think I was quite frustrated in the beginning at not being able to represent my sound and what I thought I could add to the scene. Because I wasn't there I didn't get exposed to what was going on. What I could see was people who were excited to hear new music, so I kept picking up tunes, ready to keep on sharing my music. Unfortunately, I wasn't able to do that through the newly emerging club scene, so I had to create my own path. I had to create something that was separate to Paul and Nicky and Danny. I was now very much on the outside of all of that.

Spectrum at Heaven had created a foothold for acid house in the West End and venues started looking for promoters and DJs to put on their own parties, but this mostly didn't work out as the scene was initially small and centred around a bunch of key individuals. Heaven as a venue worked well because the staff knew how to look after a crowd that were there to dance. Mainly known as a gay club, Heaven was the brainchild of Jeremy Norman, who'd been to Studio 54 in New York and Studio One in LA and brought the concepts back to the UK. He could see how important the DJs were to the scene there and brought Ian Levine in as his DJ to help shape the sound. At the time when acid house was looking for a home, Jeremy had a licensed warehouse-style venue with an epic sound system that was ready and waiting.

I managed to get a slot there in early '88, not on the main floor but upstairs. Playing anywhere was good enough for me and I worked the crowd hard. It was there that I came to meet some of the promoters of the future rave scene. London was a melting pot and acid house spread across the UK and around the world. There were lots of regional scenes that were linked to what was going on in the big urban centres, in particular Manchester and London. Promoters became more adventurous and the ones that put a lot of effort into their nights reaped the rewards. One of my favourites was a guy called Eddie, who ran the Empire in Bognor Regis. His parties were superb, and he always looked after us DJs, which made us tell all our mates and want to go back there. There's nothing worse than rocking a full club and then being made to wait until 6am to get begrudgingly given £100 and then watch a promoter jump into his BMW and zoom off.

But there was something else around the corner that emerged from the new acid house scene – a far bigger scene that I could sink my teeth into and that would embrace me with open arms. A scene that would shake the foundations of the music industry and society, send shockwaves through Middle England, and capture the imagination of a whole generation looking to make their mark. It was the dawn of a new age and the age was rave. If the new acid house club scene was the advance guard, rave was the full-on invasion force.

People wanted to party but the tough licensing laws meant there was nowhere to go. Very soon after Shoom, Spectrum and Nicky Holloway's Trip at the Astoria came a mass movement of young people looking for the next party. These parties needed a location, but above all they needed DJs and sound systems. Hello!

I was already on the frontline for these events as a main ticket outlet on the South Coast. The rave organisers like Sunrise and Tintin Chambers' Energy were hiring in massive amounts of production. Most flyers would bill the amount of turbo sound and lasers as prominently as the DJs. They needed more and more sound and they needed reliable ticket sellers. I had a brainwave. I'd only agree to push these events if I could DJ and be paid to DJ. At the beginning I know I only got booked and paid because I brought people along. In the days before mobile phones and social media it was all about distributing flyers and word of mouth. I started off as the warm-up to the warm-up, but I used to smash it every time I played, so even though there were all these famous guys playing after me I was being pushed further and further up the bill. From 10pm toward midnight, and then at 3 or 4am when people were arriving from clubs. People started to expect something special from me and I tried not to disappoint. I put more and more into my sets.

I wasn't really playing anywhere else regularly so I would put everything into delivering to the rave crowd. I knew I was playing in a way that no one else was. Danny Rampling calls my style 'ferocious' because I attack the decks with all I've got. I just wanted to push myself further and further – I was sure that this art form was in its early days and that there was more to it than just programming and mixing. At one rave I carried on playing until 10am and it was here that I did something that would change my career and – I believe – the perception of what a DJ actually does.

At a big event there would often be a spare deck on the side in case one went down. You'd be on the one's and two's and having a spare was essential, especially as it was likely that if something went wrong the sound guy would have already disappeared into the middle of the dancefloor frenzy and even if you did find him he'd be in no fit state to help out.

I was rocking it – I could feel the energy back from the crowd and I felt like I had more to say, a lot more. Every top DJ was there and I was still quite unknown but felt I was ready to step up. There were over 15,000 people still there and Maxine, my girlfriend and manager at the time, looked at me and said, 'There are three decks there, you know you can do it.' Caught up in the moment, I stuck a record on the spare deck and mixed it in. The sound was fatter than I had imagined it could be and, as most of my sets are unplanned, it wasn't difficult to keep going. It was like slow motion for me as I pulled out my records. I had two copies of 'French Kiss' by Lil Louis and I mixed in the a capella of Doug Lazy's 'Let It Roll'. The crowd had been winding down, ready for the journey home, when the music hit them. It was as if I had just re-energised them with this magical sound as 15,000 people found the hidden reserves to get back on the dancefloor.

Suddenly I had the extra platform to generate the deepness to my set that I'd been looking for. People were amazed and party goers and promoters alike came over to see what was going on. The word spread like wildfire around the party and groups of ravers came over to see what the newly christened 'Three Deck Wizard' was up to. Maxine handed out my business card to all the promoters and said, 'If you want to book him, his name's Carl Cox,' and that was it. The cork was definitely out of the bottle and nothing was going to get it back in. The Three Deck Wizard was born and I was suddenly a somebody in the DJ world. I never looked back.

I could see what was making me stand out from the other DJs. Creating the atmosphere with my records was always the essence of what I was doing. So when I was mixing between two records in my unique style people were really responding to something that they weren't getting anywhere else, and when I'd drop in that extra tune to my three-turntable sets it would take people to another planet.

When I wasn't playing at a rave I was going to one. A big part of the rave experience was trying to find the party. We travelled in convoys, sent on our mission by flyers, radio stations and word of mouth. We'd converge from all across the UK, normally arranging to meet at a service station on the M25. Sometimes the instructions weren't clear and sometimes the party was cancelled but the thrill of the chase still made it fun. There were times when I spent the whole night going round and round without finding the party. I used to drive a minibus most of the time as I was also selling tickets to the events. I was the go-to guy on the South Coast for rave tickets and would include the coach fare in the overall price. I used to work in a record shop in Brighton called Mi Price. This gave me access to the newest sounds and also was a handy place for people to pick up their rave tickets. I felt like my finger was as firmly on the pulse as anyone's could be. As well as being a DJ, I was a ticket seller working in a record shop selling the latest tracks to people who'd hear them at the parties I was at.

One track that sticks in my mind from my Mi Price days was called 'Yaaah' by D-Shake. I heard Fabio play it on a Friday at the Brighton Centre and from the first cry of 'Make some noise' and the crowd's reaction I knew it was going to be big, so I left a message on the answer machine of the record company and by the time I opened up on Saturday mid-morning I had fifty copies which all went that day. It's a great tune that still sounds fantastic today.

We also sold mix tapes, normally bootlegs from the various raves. None of us minded the mix tapes to start with as we considered them to be free promotion. None of the DJs made a penny out of them but we thought of them as a part of the scene. I'd be working behind the counter of the record shop and someone would come in and buy a Carl Cox mix tape, with all the money going to the record shop and to the person who brought in the tapes, normally a sound engineer from the party. It never occurred to me that we should have been paid, and for that matter that the artists we played should also get paid. We were selling hundreds of tapes every week and if you multiply that by every record store, market, car boot and rave, you can see why the record companies saw pound signs and started releasing their own dance music compilations.

By 1990 I was now headlining and my name was out there. I was on the flyers alongside the big names from the scene. It seemed like one minute I had my name on a bit of paper behind the decks at Shoom as I played to 200 people, the next thing it's on posters all across the country as I played to 20,000 people. At first the promoters weren't quite sure how to bill me. You normally put something after the DJ's name to explain where the DJ had come from. For example, for the Love Dove Dance 1 'Mother of all Night Raves' that the flyer proclaimed had 'The Greatest line-up of DJs ever assembled in the UK' they billed the support DJs as Nicky Holloway ('Pasha & the Milk Bar'), Kiss FM's Colin Dale and Grooverider & Fabio (from Rage). The first headliner was easy: 'From Radio One & the Milk Bar', Pete Tong.

Then it was my turn. I wasn't playing anywhere of note regularly so there was no reference point for the punters. They had to know me by name and reputation; I didn't have a venue or radio station to stand alongside. I don't know how and where the name started, but I was billed as 'The People's Choice', Carl Cox. And that became my regular billing. People were asking promoters to book me and wouldn't buy tickets unless I was on the bill. I've heard stories of people spending weekends driving around looking for the rave that Coxy was playing rather than going to something local. 'People's Choice' – I liked that. It made me feel wanted.

You'd see the same faces out and about and we were all having fun. The weekends were one long continuous party where people from all backgrounds, races and sexes came together to dance. Ecstasy was part of the scene and had brought all these people together in a way that the Establishment couldn't understand. People just wanted to be happy, connect and dance. There wasn't any dark, murky undercurrent – it was just people having a blast. The Summer of Love that really kicked off in '88 was all about freedom, with acid house as the soundtrack and baggy clothes as the uniform. Like most youth movements and their style tribes over the last fifty years, from rockers to mods and goths to ravers, we were 'all individuals' who just happened to dress, look and act in a similar way.

The rave scene was all about discovering your night. There was a lot involved just to find out what was going on and getting access to a ticket, especially as you often had to go through the act of becoming a member of the particular organisation first. Once you were on the way to the party you didn't know exactly where you were going, who you were going to meet, what was going to happen and what music you would hear.

You just knew that every week you were embarking on something really exciting that could change your life forever. And for many of us it did.

People say that if you can remember what you were doing in 1988/89 then you weren't there, but the people who say that were in fact *not* there. Anyone who was part of that magical time cannot forget the experiences and adventures they had. The stories from the rave scene are numerous and mostly end with a big smile. My late afternoons were mostly spent driving around trying to give the police the slip on the way to a rave or driving around acting as a decoy. The rest of the night would be a mixture of playing music and raving alongside thousands of people. I didn't miss many parties and was at nearly all of the great ones. The only one I wished I'd been at was the legendary Boy's Own one where Cymon Eckel and Terry Farley created this magical experience surrounded by giant hay bales and where a flock of geese, as if part of the show, took off from a nearby lake as the sun came up.

Of course, at this early stage it was still very hit and miss. Fortunately, more hit than miss, but there were a couple of real duds. I think it was New Year's Eve 1988 and I was booked to play at a big party in Lincolnshire. A few of us turned up and I got my records out of the car and headed to the venue to discover there was no one there. Well, not quite no one - the promoter was there with his close family, but that was it. He had decided to promote the event through word of mouth only, but had then kept his mouth shut and neglected to tell everyone about the party. He looked like he wanted to throw himself off a bridge, and in those days you'd only get paid from the ticket money, so this was a long trip for nothing. In case you're wondering, I actually played for his family until about a quarter past midnight so they could see in the New Year together. There I was, the Three Deck Wizard, playing deep house and techno to ten people on the dancefloor. The promoter didn't crack a smile all night but at least his granny and auntie enjoyed themselves!

Compared to this next booking that night was a success. Maxine had been telling all the promoters that they needed to book me as a DJ in order to use my sound system, and I was so busy that I was actually getting other sound systems to cover the events I couldn't reach out to. Maxine was a big part in getting me out there and building my name across the entire UK by booking me at show after show after show. Sometimes I was doing three gigs per night and 99 per cent of the time they were amazing. Not great for the relationship, as it turned out, but great for the career.

Normally you only work with promoters you know because you want to make sure the event is up to scratch, that everyone involved will get paid and that the party goers have a great time. The thing about the fledgling scene was that until you'd worked with a promoter once you didn't really know much about them. One of these 'gigs' is what we now call the Abergavenny Mystery. It was the very early 1990s and I was booked to play a party at what I thought was Abergavenny Town Hall. The booking had come through as normal with a fee agreed and set times all worked out. Maxine would have had a good chat with them on the phone to make sure it was worth going to and I think the fact that it was in a town hall reassured us that this event wouldn't be stopped. It was a long drive, about four hours to get there, so I set off on the Thursday afternoon. When I got to the address it wasn't actually the town hall, it was the Abergavenny Scout hall! This wouldn't have been a problem except that it was closed and locked and clearly not expecting a Carl Cox rave. I was searching out payphones in Abergavenny to try and see if I was at the wrong place or there on the wrong day, but I couldn't get an answer from anyone. I went back to the Scout hall, which seemed even more closed than before – there was nobody there. I had a couple of mates with me (including Ian Hussey, who would go on in later years to be my tour manager) and we hung around for a bit, but then finally there was nothing else left to do but drive back to Brighton. I never found out what happened that night. It could have been a practical joke or it could have been a rival promoter sending me out on a wild-goose chase. It really was and still is a mystery.

There are videos that do the rounds where DJs fall over or the decks get tipped on the ground by overzealous fans, but I never experienced any mishaps that stopped the music. I was always prepared and never left the house without the tools of my trade: the latest acid house, techno, rave breaks and jungle tracks as well as three slip-mats and my headphones. There was this one time which I think is my ultimate blooper moment. I was booked to play at an indoor rave in Gravesend and was running late. I was sitting in the back of the car with the records and when we hit the town I realised I couldn't remember what the venue was called. We drove around in a panic when luckily we saw a sign with the word 'Rave' on it and an arrow. We followed the arrows until we came to a massive pub that was holding the rave. The place was packed, with big queues outside, so I grabbed my boxes and made my way straight to the stage. The resident was nearly through his set and as I approached he made way for me and I pulled out my first tune, ready to mix straight into his. Big cheer from the crowd and it's on. There were a couple of nervous-looking promoter types hanging around but I had a crowd to rock so just got stuck in.

Turned out that I wasn't meant to be there at all. The resident had assumed I was as I turned up with boxes of records and the crowd thought I was the 'surprise guest' advertised on the flyer. The promoters came over and said they hadn't booked me and it was then that I realised the party I was meant to be at was on the other side of town and that I was playing at the wrong rave. I played a couple more tracks before mixing back into the resident and leaving.

Looking back at the whole scene now it still seems very chaotic but the Energy parties seemed to be able to navigate through the craziness. I think many of us thought that rave was a short-term thing, so these guys went all-out to deliver the best parties possible. I remember one event we had in Effingham in Surrey on a Bank Holiday weekend. The police had made a half-hearted attempt to stop this event even though, amazingly, they had permission to make it happen. Apparently, there were a couple of police vans blocking the road that were charged by ravers led by the security team. The police all quickly got into the vans, at which point they were surrounded by people who lifted the cops' vehicles up and carried them to the side of the road, allowing the convoy to drive through to the rave. This story might well be an urban legend, but I've seen several similar things with my own eyes. Other rave promoters that weekend were not so lucky and the police closed a lot of parties down. When a party was closed down you had to pay back the ticket holders, and if you didn't your reputation was over. That weekend, Tintin and his partner Jeremy Taylor were getting calls from desperate promoters and started to get ticket holders of cancelled events turning up at theirs. They ended up with 20,000 people having the time of their lives.

As the scene expanded so quickly, it did lead to some problems that, due to the nature of the scene, we had to tackle from within – we couldn't exactly call the police. Not understanding what's involved in promoting an event, some people try to jump on the bandwagon, seeing it as a way to earn easy cash. These fly-by-nights would falsely advertise artists that were never gonna be there, and when they did actually have a rave-scene headliner they would pay over the odds at the expense of the rest of the line-up and production. Suddenly it wasn't just about whether you would find the rave but whether the rave would be any good when you got there. If you think about it, how many times would you go to an event that didn't exist before you stopped bothering to go out at all?

We were working very hard, travelling all around the country and building a whole scene from scratch. By 'we', I mean a group of DJs who would run into each other at different events; we all knew we were part of something. The rave scene was running parallel to the club scene inside licensed premises. I missed out on the first wave of acid house clubs, which is why I had ended up so active in the rave scene, but I was now starting to get invited to play in clubs as well. Promoters and club owners had realised that if my name on a flyer could bring 20,000 people to a rave, it could probably bring 500 people to a club. The clubs started to entice the DJs into the clubs by offering them the same kind of money or more than they were getting at the raves. The trouble was, with the smaller capacity, the clubs had to charge more, so the impression it gave was that the DJs were ripping off their fans. I started my weekly night at the Zap club in Brighton and we only charged £5 on the door. I had great support from fellow DJs like Dave Angel, Sasha and Fabio - all playing for the love. The club were quite relaxed and treated the clubbers with respect, although they did make me put on the flyers that 'Persons with visible tattoos will not be admitted'. Finally, I was doing things the way I wanted. Brighton had been very good to me and now I wanted to give something back.

Brighton had a great scene and I was at the heart of it. The town still has a really happening club life but during the golden age of rave it was at its most fantastic. I was really lucky to be living there, there was always somewhere to go and something to do. Being close to London, the flyers would often end up in London's record shops, so my name was out there at places like Fat Cat, Unity and Blackmarket. Sitting alongside the rave flyers were those for licensed parties. I played at the first Passion all-nighter at The Event in Brighton in September 1992, which ran from 9pm until 7am. They pulled out all the stops and I was joined by Grooverider, Eddie Richards, Jumping Jack Frost and Fabio. Afterwards it was back to the beach for some more tunes. The beach in question was Black Rock, which had become the unofficial Coxy After Party. It all started at the end of 1987 when I started playing at the Zap club on the seafront in Brighton. Thursday night became my regular night and every second week, after the club closed, at 3am I'd head down the coast to Black Rock where I'd set up a sound system and play until the sun came up. This was a free party in the open air for about 200 people looking for somewhere to go and carry on dancing. We never gave out the exact address, it was just 'up the road and you'll hear us'. This was proper underground and ran solidly until 1989 when it was shut down. After that I'd do the odd one, normally after a big gig, and then it was only for those in the know.

I remember the first time that I realised I had become famous. It was 1991 and things were going really well. Of course, I knew that in the dance music world everyone knew who Carl Cox was, but I didn't know that this had spread much wider. I decided to splash out on a holiday and booked to go to the Maldives. That was about as far away from the rave scene as you could possibly get. I wouldn't know anyone there and for sure they wouldn't know me.

Day one, I'm in the pool when I hear, 'Carl, what are you doing here?' I looked over and there was a smart couple - at least, I think they were smart, even though it's hard to tell when they're wearing swimming costumes - and they waved me over. It turned out they didn't know me at all, but used to see me at the odd rave or two. Then they asked me for my autograph. This had never happened before. I mean, I wasn't on the telly or in a band or a footballer, I was just Carl Cox from Carshalton. I scribbled my name on something waterproof and remember feeling a little bit embarrassed. I hoped it looked OK.

So we were all standing in the pool and it was a little bit awkward, so I turned around and waded to the other side, and as I did - and this is the bit that has stuck with me for all these years - I heard the wife say to her husband: 'I can't believe it's really him, we've just met Carl Cox!'

*

As the rave scene grew my style moved towards a breakbeat-meets-techno sound, which people found hard to categorise, so they just let me do my own thing without giving me a label that I would have to stick to. This meant I could move easily between various events with the crowd knowing that I played my music my way. No matter where I was the crowd seemed to get off on my style. I was playing at Nemesis '91 in May at the Granby Halls Leisure Centre in Leicester on a bill which was very beat-heavy and included Top Buzz, Grooverider, DJ SS and DJ SY as well as a live PA from the Prodigy, and I worked a couple of house gens into my set to watch the crowd go mental. The party was from 8pm to 8am and the crowd were really up for everything. The Prodigy were the standout live band on the scene and we'd often be on the same bill. A couple of months earlier I'd played 'Everybody in the Place' at a club in London and Liam Howlett had come running over to tell me that was the first time he'd heard a DJ play his music out.

There are so many incredible stories about the parties and raves that I imagine some of the people reading this are worried that I might name-check them. No need to worry, we were all having fun and we all have our own memories that we carry with us. One of my best nights, possibly the best night ever, was the White Waltham rave in 1989. I had two coachloads of party people following me up from Brighton as we looked for the party. As was the norm, we suddenly got into a convoy and started following all the other revellers heading to the rave. I think we were all following some random car because after an hour of snaking through country roads, we ended up in a cul-de-sac - and I don't mean a dead-end, I mean a nice, smart, residential street that suddenly had several hundred ravers in coaches pulling in and then trying to do U-turns to get out. You could see the lace curtains being pulled back all around as the residents looked out in fear and wondered what was going on. Luckily, all the U-turns were done smoothly and the talk of setting up a sound system in the street and having a party there came to nothing.

By the time we got to the rave, it was 2am. I think it was organised by Energy and I was definitely playing there. It was an incredible party with amazing production and all of us seasoned ravers felt that this was what a good party should be: a friendly and respectful crowd dancing together. It's amazing how looking at things from a different perspective can paint a different picture. Come Monday morning, the newspapers were writing about this party in the way that only the British tabloid press seemed to be able to do. They made out that this was the worst party of all time and that the 'acid house ravers' were deranged animals. They showed photographs of the inside of the warehouse at the end of the rave and strewn all over the ground was rubbish and bits of paper. They made out that these hundreds and thousands of pieces of paper were what they called 'ecstasy wrappers', and the dead pigeons that were lying on the ground were apparently part of some crazed drug thing. They talked about birds with their heads bitten off, surrounded by drugs wrappers.

This story is told a lot and I can tell you exactly what this was. The birds, of which there were probably five or six were just dead birds in a warehouse that the local stray cats hadn't got to yet. Do you really think that we would want to dance on dead birds? Of course not. We'd rather dance *with* birds! As regards the 'drugs papers', they were actually the paper from the confetti cannons that had been blasted across the dance-floor by the promoters. The journalists knew this full well and

I remember seeing a couple of people taking pictures at the end. I don't regret much, but if I had a time machine, I'd go back to that party, take that photographer and show him the inside of the confetti cannon, which would then enable him to get a proper bird's-eye view of the dancefloor as I launched him through the roof of the warehouse.

From the simple 'Oi! Oi!' to the more blatant 'What's your name? Where are you from? What are you on?' and to Gary Haisman's immortal cry of 'Acieeed!' we had our own language and it felt like this could and should go on forever. Of course, once the papers started to pick up on the story the writing was on the wall. The *Sun* newspaper had originally seen everything as a bit of fun, even selling their own Acid Smiley T-shirt range, but after pictures of convoys of cars on the way to illicit raves and stories confusing acid house with acid and LSD the tide turned. OK, so these raves were pretty harmless, non-violent gatherings where young people danced, but the powers that be weren't getting their slice so surely the kids must be up to no good. Enter the Pay Party Unit.

The Pay Party Unit was a task force set up to stop the raves dead in their tracks. They didn't even think of trying to control them – their brief was to shut them down. They deployed all sorts of methods, from trying to find out where the parties were, to following the promoters and DJs, but while the city cops were relatively sophisticated in their approach the rural police were out of their depth. A village policeman on a bicycle with a whistle is not going to have an easy time telling 10,000 ravers who suddenly appear on his doorstep to turn the noise down. The rural strategy involved being on the look-out for gates with broken locks, trucks pulling generators and lots of people gathering on petrol-station forecourts. But no matter how clever the police thought they were, the promoters, even the amateur ones, were always one (or two) steps ahead.

I had my own run-in with the Pay Party Unit. It's a story that not many people know I was involved with, as I've hardly ever spoken about it. The PPU's mission was to track down acid house parties and raves, and they basically identified me as someone to follow on the weekend to see where I'd end up. I was told they'd tapped my phone and they were definitely parked outside my place, so I had to talk in code to anyone about where I was going, what I needed and when I would be there. I had a hire van that was a branded Fiat Panda, so whenever you saw the Panda van you knew it was Carl Cox. Thinking about it now, I should have probably hired a different van every so often.

This whole gig business was a bit haphazard. Someone you knew or a mate or even a mate of a mate would book you. You'd turn up and play and then get paid. Sometimes you didn't get paid because the promoters didn't have enough money or had vanished before the end, and sometimes you'd turn up and there'd be no rave, like at Abergavenny. You had to make a judgement call and go with your gut instinct, and nine times out of ten it would work out, more or less. This time I got it wrong.

It was a party where nobody knew who the promoters were. I remember it was called Space and thinking that was a great name for a party. As it turned out, they were all undercover police. We didn't have a clue, I mean who'd have believed that anybody would think this was a good strategy. It was probably called something like Operation Big Fish. It was the police who had booked the sound system from me, the lighting, the bar, everything. It wasn't cheap, and it was all from police funds.

The party was full of new faces and what we didn't realise was that most of the people we were talking to and hugging were undercover police. They needed to justify the amount of money they had wasted on trying and failing to stop the raves and came up with this plan to capture all the so-called 'acid house kingpins' in one go. As the party progressed – and, to be fair, the police seemed to know how to throw a kicking party – they suddenly stopped the music and started grabbing and searching everyone. It went from hands in the air to 'hands up'.

They totally missed what acid house was all about and, needless to say, they caught us with nothing. No one had anything on them they shouldn't have. They believed we were selling drugs, but by the time they busted the party there were no drugs to be found on anyone. They didn't let that stop them. They kept us overnight in jail until Monday morning, when we went to court in the same clothes we'd been raving in. Even though we must have looked a sight, the charges were thrown out straightaway as they didn't have sufficient evidence against us. That was the last we heard of the police.

Unfortunately, they had tipped off the tabloid press, who were relishing making up stories about the 'kingpins' and 'drugs barons' corrupting the sweet and gentle youth of the UK. At the end of the day I walked out of the court with my head held high, but when I read the headlines in the newspapers I was like 'What!' I couldn't believe what they were making up about me; it definitely affected my confidence, especially around close friends and family.

The whole case came to nothing, although it did damage my career a little bit in 1989. Being labelled a 'kingpin' is nothing like being called a 'king'. My wedding business tailed off, which it would have done in any case, and some promoters became nervous to book me having read the papers, feeling that I might bring unwanted heat on them. What changed for me was how I approached bookings after this. Firstly, from then on I'd never just turn up but had to be properly contracted to be at someone's event. Whatever it was, there would have to be a contract there for me and I wouldn't go unless I got all of the money up front. This was turning into a proper business, with proper events, which meant punters with tickets and us being at the sites and venues with permission.

It was around this time that corporate elements started to take an interest in what we were doing. By 1990 I was known to most of the record companies and was starting to get bookings through them supporting various artists. Lenny Dee from New York was brought over to play alongside me in support of Guru Josh on a national tour. We would be the warm-ups and would then play after the main performance. I didn't enjoy the tour, feeling that we were suddenly somewhere between a pop act and a travelling disco, and I couldn't see how this would move the scene or my career forward. The best part was spending time with Lenny. His power and energy was amazing and watching him move effortlessly between pure hardcore and techno was a joy to behold. We'd taken it for granted that the UK was the pioneering centre of dance music and – while we had definitely developed something world class – we had forgotten that the Americans were not just sitting idly by. They were developing their original sounds and honing their skills so that when they came over to the growing rave audiences in the UK they gave us masterclass after masterclass that inspired a whole generation to get out there and make music.

I prided myself on having music that no one else had. In the early days I relied on these tunes; it was only later that

I let my skills do the talking. I remember one night in 1990 when I was playing at the Crazy Club at the Astoria where I finished my set at 4.30am. Matthew B, who would go on in the not-too-distant future to become known as Bushwacka, had just arrived from the Park in Kensington to take over and he came on with an acetate dub plate of a track that I'd never heard before and that brought the house down. It had these crazy stabs and breakdowns and I kept asking Matthew what it was but couldn't understand what he was saying. I knew I needed that record, so ended up dancing at the club until 6am when he finally finished so that I could learn that the track was by A Homeboy, A Hippie and A Funki Dredd. That's what it was like, we were all hungry for new music.

There is one part of the rave experience that is overlooked and that is the DJ's journey from the car to the stage. In all the excitement around the stories of the scene this epic struggle is often overlooked. Today, things are easy. You turn up at a festival and you have a map and a wristband and are directed by the production team straight towards your stage, probably parking right behind it. Back in the day there was no road map, you were on your own. More often than not it was dark and the ground was muddy as you tried to get from your parked car to the stage. By the time you found the stage you were probably covered in mud and the key was to protect the records, your trainers and your clothes – in that order.

I remember this one time when it nearly went terribly wrong. It was December 1992 and I was headlining for Universe at In The Underworld near Exeter in Devon. It was cold and wet and the sell-out crowd, who'd come to dance to an all-star line-up including Fabio, Mickey Finn, Tanith, Colin Dale, Kenny Ken and N-Joi, had churned the ground up. I had on a brand-new pair of Adidas and as I tiptoed through the mud I slipped over and went down. I tried to lift my record boxes towards my body and somehow ended up doing a sort of forward roll. I was absolutely covered from head to toe but the record boxes were clean. I was with a couple of friends and pretty soon they'd also gone over. We made it to the front of the stage and had to decide whether to go left or right to try to get backstage. We made the wrong choice and it was only after a couple more falls that we made it to the stage. The security just looked at us and waved us through. This was in the days before dressing rooms so I had to crouch down with a bottle of water and the inside of my T-shirt to try to clean myself off. Face and trainers were passable and I climbed up on stage wearing a Universe T-shirt and flight jacket that I'd just been given.

Most people think of raves as something illegal, but as the venues started to realise that they could reach capacity with a much higher than the normal ticket price, which made up for people not drinking, they welcomed the promoters with open arms. One of the most important venue hosts was the Eclipse in Coventry. I was playing at all the biggest raves like Telepathy and Perception, which were in the open air, so playing indoors for a totally up-for-it crowd was something new. You didn't need to look over your shoulder because this wasn't an unlicensed warehouse where the padlock had mysteriously fallen off the gate as the doors swung open, it was a place with a proper licence.

The Eclipse was a former bingo hall that had a 16,000 capacity and, because of its location and size, attracted trusted promoters. I don't mean trusted by the venues - they didn't have a clue what was going on - but by the DJs who knew they would have a good night and also get paid, as well as the ravers who knew that the party and the party people would be awesome.

In April 1992 I headlined at Energy at the Eclipse, which was the same night that the ITV show *The Hitman & Her* were filming there. For those that don't know, the show was hosted by music producer Pete Waterman and kids' TV presenter Michaela Strachan, and it would normally come from your typical Ritzy-style nightclub, playing the chart hits of the day. Now, not a lot of people know this, but Pete liked acid house and could see similarities between how we use technology in the clubs and what he did in the studio when making hit records. His brain must have gone into overdrive when he realised there was a whole market of potential music buyers who would be interested in faceless electronic music.

Normally, there would be a lot of chat between the hosts as they talked about the music and focused on the clubbers who were out at the local high-street disco having a good time. Being at Energy was like being in a whole new world. I played hard and had an MC alongside me. People didn't dance together, they danced TOGETHER! It was basically a full-on rave experience indoors and on TV. People watching this at home across the UK must have felt they were at a rave and, with very little commentary or interviews, you could really get into it. They interviewed a few dripping-wet ravers, who were all over the place. Michaela Strachan looked like she was having fun but was clearly thinking that the people were bonkers to pay twenty quid for this. Of course, they were bonkers, but not in the way she thought, and she famously commented that 'It's too hot . . . they've all got eyes like saucers.' As the show progressed you got the occasional glimpse of Pete Waterman looking more and more bedraggled and covered in sweat.

There was so much new music to absorb that most of the DJs became serious vinyl junkies. From club hits, white labels and test pressings to imports and bootlegs we were spoilt for choice. For me the stand-out tune of the whole rave era was 'Move Your Body' by Xpansions, which came out in 1990. It fused acid, house and breakbeat and had hypnotic lyrics that were perfect for the scene. 'Move Your Body' was a massive Eclipse anthem.

Clubs like the Eclipse in Coventry and The Warehouse in Plymouth brought the rave scene into town centres, whereas before it had mainly been in fields in the middle of nowhere. Local resident DJs like Parks and Wilson at the Eclipse became local celebrities. It was cool to be up and out all night. The walk of shame had become the walk of fame. We had come a long way and a scene was slowly legitimised as the commercial possibilities became evident. These clubs should have stayed at the centre of every town forever. Sadly, the Eclipse is now a car park! I guess some people would call that progress.

The following summer I was back on stage with Universe at what would turn out to be a historic event. By 1993 there were a few stand-out promoters like Raindance, who had thrown the first legal all-night rave in September 1989 at Jenkins Lane in east London, but the crackdown on the unlicensed rave scene was taking its toll, with more parties being stopped than not and with sound systems being impounded. Big Love in August 1993 on a farm in Wiltshire was billed as Universe's last party of the year and they pulled together a dream line-up at this licensed event that would turn out to be the last totally outdoor event in the UK. The DJs included Frankie Knuckles, Paul Oakenfold, LTJ Bukem, Laurent Garnier, DJ Dag, Lenny Dee, David Morales and me. On the live front they had the

Prodigy, Aphex Twin and my live show, Carl Cox Concept. The party ran from midday until 9am with 30,000 party people coming together in positivity, and it should have showed that we were a proper industry, something to be proud of.

We felt that if we could make this into its own industry we would be taken seriously. It made sense to us. By going legit we felt that we were winning the police and the government over. Surely it meant we weren't going to get busted and could make this scene something that everyone could be proud of. We had done it!

Little did I know that we would nearly manage to screw it up ourselves and that the Criminal Justice Bill was just around the corner.

5.

Tripping Up

We had it all. A scene of our own with the music we loved, and hundreds of thousands of people moving to its beat every weekend. The rave scene had started as a small movement with for those in the know – 'Oi! Oi!' – and had grown into a scene that was dominating clubbing and driving youth culture globally. It was the most amazing time in a lot of people's lives and I was a big part of it.

At the start I was on the sidelines, but still close to the edge of the pitch, and before long I was at the very heart of it. The Second Summer of Love that ran from 1988 until about 1991 brought everyone together and I was learning more and more about the power of music and how to improve myself behind the decks. We felt unstoppable and that all the hard work was paying off.

Then we nearly threw it all away. We went from the Summer of Love to the end of rave in five short years. We tripped over our own dancing feet and it seemed we were about to fall flat on our faces.

To most people the whole acid house thing seemed to come out of nowhere. Even for those of us at the forefront the growth took us by surprise. When I played on the opening night of Shoom I couldn't have imagined what was about to happen. Dressing to impress was out and the baggy look was in. People went out to dance and sweat, so oversized T-shirts and dungarees made sense. Not since punk had music and fashion become so important, but while real punk only lasted a couple of years we are still riding the dance music revolution today. Dance music is for everyone and us early ravers were discovering this from scratch. As the first generation of the movement, we were our own guinea pigs. We believed we were doing something important. And we were right. Looking back now I can see that we were sowing the seeds for a forest that is still growing strong. We were using music to help bring everyone together, no matter who they were. Chelsea girls danced with East End boys and hardened football fans danced with hairdressers. You could see society shifting as black and white and straight and gay all danced together. It was happening right in front of my eyes and I loved it.

For me, the whole thing started in London. Future, Spectrum, the Trip and Shoom were the places on everyone's lips. I'd been at the Project Club with Paul Oakenfold and Trevor Fung after their famous Ibiza holiday and I'd seen the legendary Alfredo in action when he came to play there. All the DJs were learning on the job, but I had a secret weapon. I'd been entertaining people with my records since I was eight and had already developed a style based on having to keep the dancefloors full of sugar-fuelled kids and pissed-up wedding guests moving. When Danny Rampling brought me in to warm up at Klub Sch-oom, which would later become Shoom, I felt that this could be my big break. It was still a word-of-mouth thing and cost £4 to get in once you knew where to go. The paper flyer told everyone what to expect: 'The plastic – hard, fast and unexpected.' Because the club was in a gym, before we could set up we had to move all the sports gear. Danny filled the place with smoke and basically there was a toilet, a bar and an area to dance. But it was ours and that's what mattered.

Danny had seen me play and picked me to open the club, then, dropped me after a fortnight, which was a real blow. Like all DJs, I was fighting for my position, and bringing in the sound system gave me an edge, but I knew that Danny wanted me for my style of playing. I was only there for two weeks before Danny replaced me as his warm-up DJ. He also replaced my sound system with Norman and Joey Jay's. I was well and truly out. Danny would go on to bring in DJs like Pete Heller, Terry Farley and Andrew Weatherall. But once you'd experienced the new sound you couldn't go back. People who weren't into this became outsiders and the 'cool' trendy clubbers suddenly looked like dinosaurs. We were all about having fun and I was all about the music. The rave scene was perfect for me. It was all about big sound and partying all night, which suited me down to the ground. The Second Summer of Love was meant to be a movement like Woodstock in the USA in the 1960s, but it was much more. Nobody thought this was going to last and nobody realised that we were building an industry. Music, drugs, fashion, art and design crashed into each other and a subculture became the defining cultural force of a generation.

After my brief stint at Shoom I was playing as much as I could and had really started to make a name for myself. There was lots of being chased around the countryside on the way to the raves but it was all part of the fun. We all rallied together at parties including Dreamscape, Energy, Helter Skelter, Sunrise, Biology, World Dance, Pandemonium, Hypnosis and EDP. I'd gone from a replaceable warm-up DJ in an old gym with a 200-person capacity to being a headliner and 'The People's Choice', playing to thousands of people every week. So when the authorities tried to regulate things we weren't having any of it.

On 27 January 1990 the 'Freedom to Party' rally had taken place at Trafalgar Square in a peaceful protest against the new anti-party laws being introduced. This was the Entertainments Act that would be passed that summer, increasing penalties on illegal raves. There were more protests all over the country. I was there, of course. I had to be to show solidarity with my fellow ravers. This was the time the media were branding me a 'kingpin', so I had to be very low-key. Now me blending in is not always easy – I know I have a distinctive look and most people there would have seen me at a rave. I made sure I was right in the middle of the crowd and surrounded by friends. I remember seeing Dave Swindells, *Time Out*'s nightlife editor, taking pictures so I made sure to put my face wherever his camera wasn't.

Telling us we couldn't party was like telling us we couldn't breathe. Raving was everything and Anton Le Pirate, part of the Energy crew and the craziest acid house dancer, was on the mic motivating us to stay united. Even I was amazed how strong we were as a collective group. Sure, I'd seen big audiences at the raves, but these party goers were following up in support of our scene and standing with us. It wasn't just about going out any more, it was a way of life, and at the core was the music. They weren't just taking the parties away – they were taking away our art.

Flyers were handed out that said, 'If the new law goes through there won't be another "Summer of Love" and there won't be any more raves, so stand up for your right to party.

Show the media and the government our strength. Are you going to let them take away your right to party?' That rally was the first time we felt we should have been taken seriously and even if the powers that be didn't respond, it was after this that licensed venues started to take note. Coventry's Eclipse opened for business in October 1990 and I could play there all night without having to join a convoy and avoid roadblocks. It was licensed and legal and I was playing to an appreciative crowd who were there to dance.

In the couple of years after the Trafalgar Square rally the whole Ibiza thing was still going strong and as the scene grew the DJs became a community. We weren't an industry yet, but I was full-time – I'd stopped all my side jobs and was making a living doing what I loved. We were getting somewhere, and DJs and promoters could be quite open about what they were doing. We still had to keep the locations of the unlicensed events under wraps, but we knew that shutting us down was impossible and the police would normally let the event finish rather than trying to break it up. We knew a lot of the police by now, we'd see them every weekend, and they could see that we meant no harm.

Castlemorton changed everything. After everything I'd put into making the scene something we could be proud of, it was a single rave that nearly finished the whole movement off. It was like no rave that had happened before and there's been nothing like it since. Some of the biggest sound systems from the warehouse scene like DIY, Bedlam and Spiral Tribe kicked it off at Castlemorton in the Malvern Hills in Worcestershire on 22 May 1992. The party was like a magnet and ended up running for a week and attracting 40,000 ravers, with little organisation. There were no loos and people were scavenging the local area for food and drinks. Huge queues at the local pay phones resulted in dealers arriving from all over the country.

This was not the scene as I knew it. It was disrespectful to the local population and didn't look after the revellers. The scale of it meant the police were powerless to do anything and the media were all over it. This party wasn't about the music, it was just somewhere to go for people who were looking for something to do. I was watching the events unfold on TV and straight away I noticed that there was very little music. It was just a giant gathering of people that had been labelled as a rave.

We'd been careful not to go too far. I just wanted to play music and entertain people and, while there were risks at the raves, they were worth taking. We'd started to make inroads into clubs and our music was getting airplay and recognition. Slowly, slowly, we were getting somewhere. Then Castlemorton - which was never even meant to be a rave, but just exploded when a group of New Age travellers were moved on by Avon and Somerset Police - painted the whole scene as a national problem that needed to be sorted out and pronto. The coverage from this event meant that questions were raised in Parliament and suddenly major legislation looked like a real possibility. The police were now out in force and the feeling of worry at every gig began to outweigh the pleasure of going. I was one of the lucky ones. I'd established a solid fanbase who followed me into the clubs and, because I'd played the big raves, I was known across the UK. Many others weren't so lucky and had to hang up their headphones, sometimes for good.

As we feared, two years later the Criminal Justice and Public Order Act of 1994 changed everything and undid all our hard

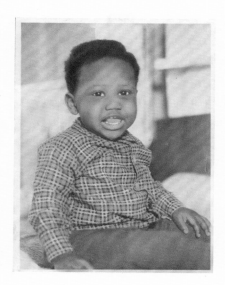

Me! © Carl Cox

My first bike – many more to come!
© Carl Cox

Me and my sisters, Pamela and Andrea – butter wouldn't melt!
© Carl Cox

Mum and Dad – miss
you and love you.
© Carl Cox

Hitting the town with my sisters.
© Carl Cox

Young DJ for hire –
no gig too small.
© Carl Cox

Mum – always with me. © Carl Cox

Dad – who gave me my first taste of music. © Carl Cox

Ultimate B.A.S.E at the Velvet Underground. © Carl Cox

Decisions, decisions! © Carl Cox

The Three Deck Wizard (at Dance Valley in the Netherlands). © Ian Hussey

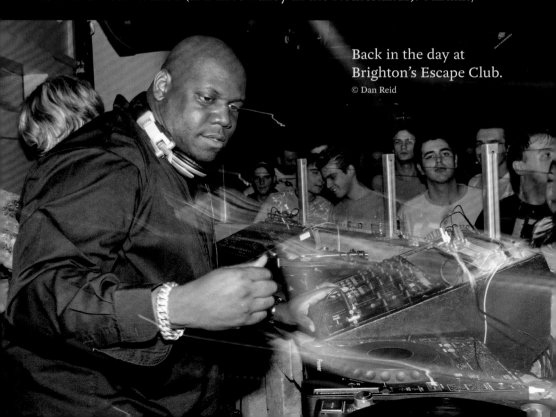

Back in the day at Brighton's Escape Club.
© Dan Reid

Feeling the energy from the crowd at Spain's Monegros Desert Festival.
© Ian Hussey

In the DJ booth at Space with Felix
da Housecat and P Diddy.
© Patrick Munoz / Courtesy of Ian Hussey

Rocking the Vote at the House of
Commons. © Dan Reid

The one and only Firestarter, Keith
Flint. © Carl Cox

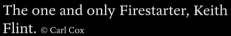

Ian Hussey going above and
beyond on tour. © Dan Reid

Berlin Love Parade in 1998. © Robert Kritsch / Philipp Straub

From wedding DJ to this! (At Stereosonic Festival, Australia.) © Ian Hussey

work. This piece of legislation was a million miles away from enjoying the freedom of dancing under the stars at Amnesia. The dreaded Section 63 was aimed at the free-party scene and gave the police the power to shut down an event if it had music that was 'characterised by the emission of a succession of repetitive beats'. I wasn't exactly sure what you could or couldn't do and I was told that four people standing outside a car and listening to dance music on the tape deck constituted a breach of the Act and could get you nicked. The police also had the power to stop any party, rave or otherwise, with over a hundred people present; they could even prevent a group of two people or more planning a rave. So unless you were going to promote, build the sound system, produce, DJ, print the flyers and sell all the tickets yourself they could close you down. They also had the power to move people away within a five-mile radius of an event if they believed they were on the way to a rave. No excuses listened to and no proof needed. We'd gone from having all the freedom we could want to this!

This was terrible for me. It was too much of a risk now for me to play at an unlicensed event. The police were confiscating sound systems; losing a couple of boxes of records would be bad enough, but losing my entire sound system would have been catastrophic. Having worked so hard to establish myself, I couldn't go back to painting ceilings.

The clubs were great, but I missed the big rave audiences and the long sets. There were a few special events that were geared up for dance music. Playing in Germany at Universe was special and a big career moment for me, but it was back home where I would be part of a party that would change everything again, this time for the better. By 1994 there was a dance tent at Glastonbury and I played alongside live acts like

Orbital. This was a special moment. Orbital smashed it. What we were doing at raves and in clubs was still seen by many as just playing someone else's records. The music industry were starting to get it but if you weren't into the scene you couldn't know that we were *creating* with our sets.

Orbital was a purely electronic dance music act that had come straight out of the rave scene. They were even named after the motorway around London that the convoys travelled on. The two Hartnoll brothers on stage sporting torch lights on the side of their workman's glasses playing original electronic music was a defining moment. I was there to DJ and played a big set - I wanted to prove what I could do. It was so hot that even when the sides of the tent went up it was like being in a club. My love affair with Glastonbury started that night, but I couldn't stop thinking about Orbital. I liked the idea of live electronic music and suddenly I could clearly see a path for me that meant I wouldn't have to rely on the strict new regulations around the rave scene.

The ravers were still trying to fight the same losing battle, showing strength in numbers with 50,000 people marching to Trafalgar Square in July and then slightly fewer, about 35,000, marching in October. October didn't end well. Fighting broke out between the protesters and the police. There was frustration on both sides, and the media were there to record it all. Unlicensed raves would never happen again on the scale that we'd seen but the powers that be had been made to sit up and take notice. They had forgotten that young people have a voice and that they need to be heard. We had deserved a slap on the wrist after Castlemorton but things had gone too far. We needed to be able to party and express ourselves, but Parliament was having none of it. Ironically, years later I would end up invited to DJ in the Houses of Parliament - but that was still a long way off.

I could see that the free party scene in the UK was over. The Prodigy's *Music for the Jilted Generation* summed up how we all felt - but the movement had grown too big to be shut down. We had to make things commercial to survive, so we began to treat things more seriously and run the events and our careers as a business, which in hindsight, was a positive move. Every music festival had a dance arena and most clubs turned their prime weekend nights over to former ravers and rave promoters. You could now walk through the centre of town with a couple of record boxes and the police wouldn't bat an eyelid. We'd nearly destroyed our own scene but had somehow emerged stronger than ever. We'd stayed true and remained underground but were now also crossing into the mainstream. Ravers became clubbers and clubbing became the number-one leisure activity for a whole generation. Rave became absorbed into the legal and licensed club and festival world as dance music became the dominant global youth culture form of expression.

6.

I Want You (Forever)

When I was growing up there was one TV show that told us what was going on in the music world and that was *Top of the Pops*. It wasn't cool or cutting-edge but it was the charts and something that we could all talk about and relate to. Back then you'd associate being No. 1 with being the best, and supporting your favourites by popping down to WHSmith's or Our Price and picking up a single was a rite of passage.

I had mates who'd be singing into a hairbrush in the mirror or strumming on a tennis racket, but for me it was always about playing records. Moving forward a few years, I was going to clubs and DJing and it never occurred to me why the records I liked and was picking up – underground early house records – were not in the charts. Looking back now with my knowledge of the industry, I can see that even the tracks that sold in large numbers were selling from the wrong kinds of shops. The record charts back in those days were compiled from sales returns from a relatively small number of shops. That's why young record company employees would be sent on missions all across the country to buy as many of their own artists' records as possible from the 'right' shops – to give them a boost in the charts.

I know some of my friends were doing this, but the charts had lost their appeal to me. Sure, there was the odd gem in there, but the stuff I wanted to hear out and about wasn't 'commercial'. Suddenly, all this changed as music started to be made by DJs. I was part of the new generation of British club goers who were turning out their own music. We were experiencing for ourselves on dancefloors what actually makes people move and were using that to create more dance music. We were making the kind of music we wanted to hear in clubs and could press up a track and have it in the hands of club DJs by the weekend. It's funny when you think about it, but dance music is often made by one person alone in a studio and, more so than most types of music, is made to be enjoyed in a group. These tracks quickly crossed over and became the anthems for our generation, like Joe Smooth's 1987 'Promised Land'.

> Brothers, sisters,
> One day we will be free
> From fighting, violence,
> People crying in the streets.
>
> When the angels from above
> Fall down and spread their wings like doves,
> As we walk, hand in hand,
> Sisters, brothers,
> We'll make it to the promised land.

This track actually is the record the most sums up Ibiza to me. It may seem a bit of an obvious choice, but you can't help smiling and getting those shivers every time you hear it.

It was one of our own home-grown DJs, the lovely super-fly guy that is Mark Moore, who went on to have the first global dance music smash hit. Mark was an influential DJ on the London club scene, playing at the WAG, the Mud Club and then at Shoom and Spectrum. He was an early adopter of house and put together, as a side project, S'Express. His 'Theme from S-Express' was a No. 1 in the UK in 1988 and went on to ride high in the charts all over the world. It was the kind of music that was made by guys who believed in what they were doing and it was played at nearly every party. It was a monster hit, but that doesn't mean it was made for commercial reasons. It was just too good *not* to be a hit. Suddenly the dance music community was everywhere - our strength in numbers was madness at that time. Anyone making that kind of music crossed over. We were really changing things ourselves and rather than us follow the music industry, they followed us.

I was playing at all the big raves and the whole scene was growing so quickly that I didn't have a choice but to grow with it. There wasn't time to even take a breath, let alone a look around. Before, I used to play at house parties, in Scout huts, I did weddings for a living. So being able to play with a proper sound system at massive venues was a privilege. Playing at all these illegal parties and being seen as someone that was at the pinnacle in making these parties work - I never thought that this would happen. It was non-stop and nationwide. I could be playing at two parties on a Wednesday, one on a Thursday, three times on a Friday, two on a Saturday with one on a Sunday to round off the week. It was incredible. I basically took it all, as much as I could to get my name out there, to promote myself as much as I could. I never thought it was going to happen but with all the hard work I put in wasn't all that surprised when it did. I continue to do that today but obviously on a much bigger scale.

Paul Oakenfold and I had stayed in close touch. By now I was a full-on rave DJ and he was a club DJ but he kept in contact – after all, he still needed his weekly money from me for the turntables! But I could see that Paul had a plan; he was making the kind of records I'd play and was reaching out way beyond the club scene. He's always had a vision and knows how to get where he needs to be. Paul was watching what I was getting up to and could see that I was taking the DJing art to another level and bringing a fusion of house, acid house and techno to audiences all across the UK.

We'd played a few gigs together. The most surreal one, and definitely the most memorable, was when we were down at Paul McCartney's farm in 1989. To avoid confusion, for the purposes of this anecdote, 'Paul' refers to Paul McCartney and 'Oakey' refers to Paul Oakenfold. So, Oakey gets a call through friends that Paul's daughter, Stella, had asked her dad if he could get Oakey to DJ for her eighteenth. You have to remember that this is rock and roll royalty and she could have had anyone she wanted – maybe even a Stevie Wonder / Annie Lennox / Eric Clapton / Sting supergroup – but she wanted Oakey. Being the kind of person he is, he didn't jump at the chance but said that he would do it if he could bring Carl Cox with him. Suddenly we were about to embark on another adventure.

I knew that Oakey wanted me there for my skills on the decks, but in the back of my mind he was also getting the van, the driver, the sound system and the decks that I was still paying him for. Nancy Noise joined us on the road trip and pretty soon we were down at the McCartney farm. The security took one look at us and got busy on their walkie-talkies. I leaned out the window and said, 'We're the DJs for Stella,' and they waved us through. Just like that!

We put up some banners, plugged in the smoke machine, connected up the turntables and the mixer and boom, away we go. I played a bit, Oakey played a bit, Nancy played a bit – we all had a great time. At the time the McCartneys had made a dance record. Linda and Paul were dancing to this record in front of us while we were playing it. I guess they are the kind of parents you wouldn't be embarrassed to have dancing at your eighteenth. Later on in the evening, Paul tapped me on the arm and invited me to have a pizza with him round the corner. I remember it as the most delicious pizza I've ever had in my life – it was a margherita with oregano and I can still taste it to this day. So there I am, spinning acid house and techno and hanging out with Paul, Linda and Stella. Stella's friends were lots of fun and they were all up for a good time. I even ended up getting a letter from Paul and Linda thanking me for helping make their daughter's dream come true.

Paul Oakenfold had started his Perfecto label in 1989, which is still going strong today, and had been listening out for my sets and following my progress. He'd heard some of my mixes and asked me about the odd track that caught his ear. I don't know if he knew I was mixing on three turntables in 1991, and when he asked me to send him a track that he'd heard I had to explain that I mixed all the elements live during my set and there was no recording. We started talking and Paul still felt this track had potential. He asked me to send him a mixed version. I remember thinking, *Why not?* I plugged in a tape recorder and made a rough version in one take using three decks, which I then dropped over to him.

Paul knew how popular I was at the time but didn't know how good my ear was. Having had a listen, he said he wanted to be part of it and booked us time in a north London recording studio. You look at it now and it's Carl Cox in the studio with legendary producer Paul Oakenfold, but back then it was just two mates having some fun. We spent the first few hours taking samples and playing with levels and then we thought we'd give it a go. Paul was surprised that I'd created most of the track myself, including the beats. The main sample was from 'Love Will Find a Way' by Victor Romeo featuring Leatrice Brown, which had come out on Jack Trax in 1989. Studio time being expensive, we decided to do the whole track live and managed to lay it down and record it in one day; by dinnertime it was pretty much down. Once I'd recorded it, I asked Paul to check it out. He listened to it a couple of times with his eyes closed while conducting in the air, and picked out a couple of tiny tweaks which we changed on the spot. We then both listened and smiled at each other. This was sounding good.

From start to finish it took a day and a half and 'I Want You (Forever)' by DJ Carl Cox was released on Perfecto. The artwork was pretty basic – lots of rave and club flyers in a collage – and it was available on seven-inch and twelve-inch. It was picked up by all the pirate stations and played out at clubs and raves everywhere. Straight away, and without any proper promo, it went to No. 1 on dance charts everywhere. Then it went into the national charts and Paul told me that *Top of the Pops* wanted me on! Now, don't get me wrong, I didn't think that I was a *TOTP* kind of act, but something about a national institution like this calling you makes you come running. The thing is, *TOTP* wanted bands and didn't really understand the concept of the DJ as an artist. We had to make a video and create a band of people to play and dance around the DJ, so we went to Pineapple studios in central London and we got a girl to sing the line 'I want you forever'. It was a sample-based record so I had to re-create the samples with live vocalists. After a few rehearsals with the singer and the dancers, we were ready.

That morning I went to get a haircut - after all, I was going on national TV. 'Haircut?!' - I can almost see your surprise. Yes, there was a time when I sported a thick head of hair. If you've seen me perform you know I give it 100 per cent and can't stop myself from dancing as I also get lost in the music. Those early warehouse parties were so hot and I'd be pouring with sweat, with it going in my eyes and dripping onto the records. I'd been toying with the idea of shaving my head but back then that look had a bit of the football hooligan about it, so I'd resisted, but on the morning of *TOTP* I thought I'd go for it. My local barber talked me out of it, saying that if I was going on TV I wouldn't want to have that as my look. Well, not long afterwards the hair came off and I've kept it shaved ever since - so much so that I almost can't remember what I looked like with it. I imagine that at this point you'll be googling me on *TOTP* and having a little giggle.

There was another more serious reason why I ended up shaving my head. When I was nineteen I'd been doing some painting and decorating and was asked to paint the ceiling of the Unigate milk depot in Croydon. I'd brought a couple of mates along with me and we set to work. There was an open pipe that had steam coming out of it and one of the lads swivelled it round, sending the steam straight across the top of my head, not realising that steam is effectively boiling water. I ended up with serious burns in several places, with the hair follicles destroyed. We did stay to finish the job before I got checked out, and Mark and Gary are still my friends to this day. From then on my hair was always a bit patchy and in 1992 I decided to go for it and shaved it all off. The other change to my look in 1992 was the glasses. I'd never worn them much while I was out, but once the hair came off I decided I'd wear my glasses every time I played so that I could see the crowd and everything around me clearly. I heard once that some people thought that with the shaved head and the glasses I was trying to look like an intellectual - clearly whoever said that didn't know me very well!

Hair and glasses were just over the horizon in 1991 as I prepared to make my appearance on *Top of the Pops*. This was it - the start of something new. All I had to do was turn up at the studio and my family and everyone else would see what I could do. Then I got a call from the vocalist to say she was sick and couldn't make it. We managed to find someone to fill in and, although she didn't really know the song, we still managed to pull it off. I've played to thousands and thousands of people but this was one of my most nerve-wracking moments, as I knew that all my friends and family would be sat around their TVs. It was great fun - the audience were into it and the dancers made it into a real show. I got to spin records on the decks and halfway through it hit me. Here I was, Carl Cox, who used to spend his pocket money on records, performing a song that I had written on the biggest music show on British television. Most artists have teams of people making everything run like clockwork, but this was really just my passion and ear coupled with Oakey's knowhow and vision that made this happen the way it did. The song ended up at No. 23 in the national charts and I'm still really proud of it.

One of the things that really helped shake the scene was that alongside the music from America we started to create our own sound. From about 1991, the hardcore sound started to dominate the raves. Having this home-grown British music scene with hundreds of thousands of people listening to it every weekend meant we started to create our own empire. The UK is a relatively small territory geographically and was being criss-crossed by a growing number of DJs supported by clubs who wanted the audience and radio stations who needed new music. Going forward, we would own the music played at the events by being the artists, owning the labels and creating our own culture. Our attitude was, if the big boys wouldn't let us play with them, we'd make them come and play with us.

The dance scene was dominated by singles. These tunes had a growing audience who could hear them in clubs and raves all week long and they would also get airplay on pirate radio stations. There had been some attempts of DJs doing albums, but without major record company support it was clear that this was a case of too much too soon. Even the likes of Frankie Knuckles and David Morales had struggled with their albums at the same time as their singles made them kings of the dancefloor. There *were* DJ albums available – you only had to go to Camden Market to find mix tapes recorded at the big raves and parties from DJs like Fabio, Sasha, Billy Nasty, Colin Dale and Dave Angel.

In 1992 we took back a little bit of control when some of the sets were officially released. The Mixmag live series was launched by DMC with a mixed album that featured Dave Seaman and myself. This meant that for the first time the track listing could also be shared with the licensing and clearances sorted out for us. People could buy a well-mastered and professionally engineered DJ set and then discover all the artists that we were playing. Suddenly, relatively unknown producers and what would have possibly been one-hit wonders in the mainstream could become artists and touring acts on the underground with a couple of dancers, a vocalist and the track on playback. As the decade progressed, DJ-mixed CDs became big sellers, with everyone from Ministry of Sound, Essential and Cream showcasing every type of dance genre to a ready and waiting market. You could walk into Tower Records and see your compilation dance CD riding high in the charts next to mainstream artists like Lenny Kravitz and Oasis.

This was all going on before we'd heard of the internet, and mobile phones were not commonplace – and they were just phones, nothing 'smart' about them. There was no Facebook, YouTube, Spotify or Myspace. If you wanted a tune you had to go out and buy it. New record shops were springing up all over the place and at any point in the day you'd find people 'digging through the crates'. The people behind the counter knew their stuff and their customers and could get a white label – a promo disc – into people's hands. They'd also slip some flyers into the bag, so were promoting the parties too. As dance music grew and the genres split into subgenres you could go to one place and pick up techno from Germany, the latest home-grown beats from James Lavelle's 'Mo' Wax' label or an anonymous track that you'd never find out who or where it came from. 'Got any jungle in, guy?'

Today, with the rise of streaming, social media and downloads, sales figures can be taken with a pinch of salt. I have millions of active followers across my various platforms, which is a great way to stay connected and spread my music, but it's not the same as the days when people had to go into a shop and choose your album over everyone else's to walk out with. It was a time when sales figures and charts helped define an entire genre and made the industry sit up and take notice. DJs were already in demand as remixers by labels and artists. In 1991, as well as being a recording artist myself, I'd remixed acts like Eternal and Art of Noise, so the industry understood the value that dance music could bring to their more mainstream roster.

It was actually an album that first made me realise that I was a big part of something special and understand how much my style and sound had crossed over from the underground to also be enjoyed by a much wider audience. It took me until 1995 to realise that I was getting through to people with my music when my *F.A.C.T.* album came out on the REACT label – it sold over 60,000 copies straightaway and then a further 200,000 copies. This was purely down to my hard work at that time, getting behind the music that I believed in and championing the sound that moved me. It was a huge number for an album like this, not really artist-driven but sound-driven. This was different to hearing it at a party and gave me the confidence that what I was doing was not only working for me but for everyone else too. That year I also broadened my remix portfolio with remixes for great acts like Jam & Spoon, The Stone Roses and Yello.

During the Second Summer of Love I'd worked hard to carve a niche for myself as a standout DJ on the rave circuit. By 1995 I was an established international DJ, a remixer, a producer and a recording artist, with the rave scene as the perfect showcase for what I was doing.

7.

Rub-a-dub-dub,
I'm in a Club!

If you pop into Tottenham Court Road underground station and stand in the ticket hall you might be surprised to learn that you're standing over a club that one night a week was given the nickname the Temple of Techno. This was the place where I held one of my most important residencies, a night that helped shape and define techno in the UK. This was the home of my Ultimate B.A.S.E.

Nicky Holloway, legendary party promoter and one of the original Ibiza Four, had opened a club on the Charing Cross Road in 1993 which he named the Velvet Underground. He opened this after his Milk Bar lost its lease. The Velvet Underground would soon be renamed the Velvet Rooms and hosted some fantastic underground nights including Fabio's Wednesday Drum and Bass night Swerve, which pioneered his new sound and vision. Later on, in about 2001, he hosted a night called FWD which you could say was the night that gave birth to dubstep.

Nicky and I were (and are) friendly and he'd unlocked the West End for DJs like me because he valued music, party people and the pioneering spirit that had given rise to acid house more than running a club as a purely commercial business. At that time getting a regular slot in town was difficult; owners didn't really understand what was going on and the press surrounding rave culture added to the reluctance of licence holders to adopt something that could cause them problems. Already the dance music community was moving in different directions, with clubbers discovering their own sounds and styles. There were some great clubs like the WAG run by Chris Sullivan and the Café de Paris but getting a slot there was almost impossible because the nights already in place were strong, with several established promoters waiting to fill any gaps. There were some venues like Maximus in Leicester Square that held regular one-offs, in this case Love Ranch, which showcased DJs like Paul Daley from Leftfield, Darren Emerson from Underworld and Andrew Weatherall from Boy's Own, who played alongside fantastic residents like Rad Rice. These weekly nights were more down to the passion of the promoters than the venues themselves and when the promoters moved on or the nights fizzled out the clubs would normally go back to what they were used to. There were always plenty of people attracted to the bright lights of town to make most venues tick over. It was only when the scene exploded to the point of no return that dance music became the dominant sound as the underground became the pulse of the entire generation.

Many of the originators of these nights would go on to shape dance culture across the UK and, indirectly, across the world. Love Ranch and the people behind it is a great example of this. This weekly club night was created by Sean McLusky and Mark Wigan, who had run the Brain Club and experimented with electronic acts there including Adamski, Orbital and A Guy Called Gerald. McLusky would go on to programme Club UK, which hosted important promoters like Universe where I played to 3,000 people who would come every Friday and Saturday to hear DJs like John Kelly, Laurent Garnier, Paul Oakenfold, John Digweed and myself in a legal, licensed, indoor rave environment. McLusky would repeat his success several times over including at the Leisure Lounge and the Complex, where he worked with Universe again on their Voyager night before moving, via a brief stint at Soho's Madame Jojo's, to The Scala. Here he transformed a derelict cinema into a live music venue where you could see anything from the Chemical Brothers and Moby to Coldplay and Roni Size.

I felt it was important for me to be seen as someone who had a headquarters, a place I could say was my 'office'. Ultimate B.A.S.E. was just that. While it sounds great to have landed this prize, it came with a price. It meant I was tied to the venue on that day of the week because that was the day people came to see you there. I was the DJ, booker, promoter and host. My Thursday night had a long and successful run, and as I picked up more and more bookings across the UK and into Europe I found myself always rushing back to the 'office'. I was pioneering my own style and sound, championing techno while incorporating interesting sounds and beats. What you begin to realise is that your core crowd wants a mixture of two things that are polar opposites. On the one side they want new underground sounds and expect you to wow them every week. On the flipside they want familiarity – those big tunes that are guaranteed to make the dancefloor go off.

I'd deliberately picked the club because I trusted Nicky to look after me and I wanted a small club where I could focus on the quality of the music rather than worrying about making lots of money from filling it with loads of clubbers. Nicky knew his way around the West End and could juggle all the background issues like making sure the security did their jobs and that the sound system was always at its best. A real plus for me was that Nicky was a DJ and had a following of real music lovers himself. I was confident that he would never compromise on the sound and the DJs playing experience; after all, he was using the same equipment from the same DJ booth as I was. I'd seen many of my friends who ran their own nights always stressing about filling the place to please the club owner and then having to play more commercial music to make the crowd happy. Of course, this would eventually alienate the real clubbing crowd they had started the night for in the first place. Nicky's principle was always music first.

The Velvet Underground held 220 people and with the licensing authorities - which basically meant the council and what we called the club squad - watching Nicky's every move it was a strict one-in, one-out door policy. This meant there was a queue outside pretty much all night long. The great thing about having your own night is that you can programme it yourself and bring in artists you want to work with. I'd set up a DJ agency called Ultimate and at the time the club was the place we could showcase all the talent we had on the books. There were three main residents - myself, Jim Masters and Trevor Rockcliffe - and between us we would take the crowd on a weekly techno-filled odyssey. I'd invite special guests to join us and because of the size of the club they were playing for next to nothing, purely for the love of music and to share their DJ vision with an appreciative audience. There is something really special about playing in what is essentially an intimate atmosphere, with condensation dripping from the ceiling as you're surrounded by waves of sound.

We also used to make sure we could share the experience with bigger crowds and so ran our Ultimate B.A.S.E. specials once a month on a Saturday night at the End, which opened in Bloomsbury in 1995. The club was the brainchild of Layo, Bushwacka! and Mr. C - another club put together and run by DJs who understood dancefloors and sound systems. It was one of my favourite places to play, with a fantastic sound system and a really eager crowd who appreciated hearing cutting-edge dance music. I was really disappointed when they finally shut up shop.

A result of having a London residency and being around on the scene was that I got to play in a lot more London clubs, which meant I could share my musical vision most nights of the week. Promoters knew I could use my sound to keep the crowd going and hopefully enhance everyone's night. I remember one night in 2003, I was DJing at Turnmills, which was run by Danny Newman and his brother Paul, who'd become an established DJ by the name of Tall Paul. They had just redecorated the club and I guess the plaster was still drying. I was in the DJ booth and really pushing that sound system to the limit when bits of the ceiling started to fall on me. I didn't really think the club would start crashing down on me, I was more worried about protecting the decks. No one else seemed to care so I just kept on going. There was even a fan dancing right in the front who was wearing an enormous Styrofoam head that had my face on it. I had such a good time that when I put on my last record I raced around to the dancefloor so I could shake my thing. Bizarrely, I ended up dancing with a massive replica of myself. It was probably the only time I could be accused of being big-headed.

I was still playing at clubs all over the country and was also going out a lot to enjoy the scene from the dancefloor. I'm not the biggest drinker, and spirits are normally my thing, but in clubland there is one place were Beer guarantees a good night and that's in Leeds. One place that's always a lot of fun is Back to Basics. Dave Beer puts his heart and soul into throwing his parties and as he was booking me in the early days I was always happy to return the favour and play for him now. It was always epic up in Leeds but I remember one particular night that stands out above the others. It was their tenth birthday, which also happened to be on Bonfire Night. I drove up and the whole way there I could see fireworks, which Dave said he'd organised especially for me. I focused on the music and delivered a blinding set while Dave and his mates got stuck into their birthday celebrations! At one point, Charlie Chester threw a birthday cake straight into Beero's face. Not a Steve Aoki-style EDM show cake but a full-on Tommy Cooper splatfest. I knew things would get messy!

The club scene in London, and I guess everywhere in the world, is pretty competitive. You want to fill the club and so does every other venue and promoter. In the pre-internet days, what people now seem to call 'back in the day', we'd promote in the only way we knew how, what the kids today call 'proper Old Skool'. It was all about flyers and word of mouth plus the odd listing in things like *Time Out*, where Dave Swindells ruled the club section and where we'd sit week after week as other nights came and went. We were lucky at Ultimate B.A.S.E. The calibre of the line-ups and the size of the club meant we were always full to capacity, so the trick for our regulars was to arrive at the right point to get straight in. Not too late when the club would be full and not too early, as it would be a long night ahead.

One night, Detroit legend DJ Jeff Mills was going to be in London so I booked him to play. Jeff is a phenomenal visionary with a relentless playing style. He is one of my favourite DJs and his sound is unequalled. I made sure to tell my friends to come early and we limited the promotion as we wanted the regulars to enjoy this. Jeff had been on tour in Japan and had absolutely smashed it – he was like a god over there, mesmerising the crowds.

Unbeknown to me, the word had got out and this night had been listed in the various nightclub sections of the magazines that catered for tourists. I turned up to the club an hour earlier than normal as I wanted to get set up before Jeff arrived. There seemed to be a much bigger queue than usual outside and I thought that most of them were probably just milling about on the pavement looking for something to do and just happened to be near the club. I kept my head down, ignoring them, and went straight in.

As soon as the doors opened, we were rammed. We were at full capacity in what was record time. It was then that I noticed that over 95 per cent of the crowd was Japanese. It was so early that not all the bar staff and security had arrived and by the time everyone was there the regulars and all my guests couldn't get in. As I said, it was one-in, one-out, and with us on the decks going for it like demons, no one was leaving early. We were taking no prisoners. I learned my lesson and when Ken Ishii came over from Japan to play, all my friends were the first in line.

It was nights like the one with Jeff Mills that helped spread the Ultimate name around the world. My reputation was growing and in the same way that we wanted the leading American, Japanese and European DJs with us, they wanted us to visit them. Ultimate B.A.S.E. parties were also taking place outside of our London home. We had a great night in New York in May 2000 when we took over Twilo and I was joined by Misstress Barbara alongside Mark Lewis, who now goes by the name Mark London. It was a great club with an unbelievably fat sound system called Phazon, which was built by Steve Dash and was totally bespoke and unique to that club. I tried to get on that system every chance I had. I did a fantastic President's Day show there in February 2001, which was billed as Carl Cox vs Danny Tenaglia. It was a Sunday night and the diehard clubbers had probably been going strong since Friday, but we showed them no mercy and kept the floor heaving until closing time.

Twilo was doing some interesting things and booking some great residencies. Sasha and Digweed had a monthly night there on the last Friday of every month that was becoming the talk of the industry. The freedom to play what they wanted in the way they wanted for an open and up-for-it crowd in a warehouse setting on that sound system was a DJ's dream. I thought to myself, *I'll be having some of that, thank you very much.* The club had already seen me in action and knew the following I'd established in New York and so offered me the first Friday of every month as Ultimate Twilo, with me, Mark Lewis and Jim Masters as the residents and with guests including Jeff Mills, Darren Emerson, Sven Väth, C.J. Bolland and The Advent already lined up.

We were all set to kick off on 3 July, but it was not to be. At the beginning of May the club was raided, officially because its Certificate of Occupancy had expired - but there were apparently also lots of licensing regulations that the owners hadn't fulfilled. We hung on, thinking that it would reopen, perhaps under another name or with new owners, but when they sold off that beautiful system we knew it was over. This was a huge disappointment, as finding a club with a system like that where I could play how I wanted was becoming rarer and rarer with landlords pushing rents up resulting in clubs not being able to invest in this kind of next-level sound system.

I'm very proud of what we achieved at the Velvet Underground. We had the best sound system in the country and played the best music alongside amazing guests including Mark Spoon, Jeff Mills, Laurent Garnier and Sven Väth. It may have only held 220 people and we might not have made any proper money, but I had the best time and shared my passion and my sound with an army of techno foot soldiers who would help us conquer the world, one dancefloor at a time.

8.

On the Shoulders
of Robots

It felt like we'd arrived. It was 1996 and the rave scene was going strong once again and, more importantly, was legal. In a short space of time, we'd gone from a tiny, localised, underground subculture to a genre that could play at festivals like Glastonbury and had shown the music industry that we could sell records and were here to stay. Tribal Gathering '96, which took place in June at Luton Hoo in Bedfordshire, was groundbreaking, and was named 'the greatest festival of all time' by *Mixmag* in 2018.

Spread across eight stages, promoters Universe brought together live acts including Chemical Brothers, Black Grape, Leftfield, Underworld and the up-and-coming Daft Punk alongside over seventy DJs including Sven Väth, Jeff Mills, Richie Hawtin, LTJ Bukem, Goldie with his Metalheadz, Darren Emerson, DJ Sneak, Sasha, Laurent Garnier, Paul Oakenfold, Armand Van Helden and myself. Starting at 1pm, it ran through until 9am the next day at a fully licensed event for 30,000 beautiful party people. The production was of the highest level with a sensory overload that saw the excitement build throughout the night. The year before had been great, with

Orbital, Moby and the Prodigy as co-headliners. But 1996 was when the word was really out. The same police that had been setting up roadblocks to stop the raves were now marshalling cars filled with ravers straight to the party. People started travelling to the UK from overseas to come to these events and I knew that this was my time to shine.

You have to remember that back then most of us DJs knew each other. We were either on the same bills or checking each other's parties out and we were meeting DJs from all over the world. Print media, TV and radio couldn't get enough of us and showcased the positive side of the scene, while having the likes of Pete Tong at BBC Radio 1 gave our fledgling industry a voice. We were learning on the job and getting influenced by each other. I've always been a hard worker and 1996 was a year I worked super-hard because I could see what was coming. We had always been chasing acceptance, but suddenly we were the ones being chased. And I don't mean like back in the day when we used all our tricks to get those parties on, I mean we were being chased by venues, promoters and record companies. We had arrived.

DJ Mag launched their top 100 and I was honoured to be the first winner chosen by public vote. At the time, *DJ Mag* was the industry bible and I felt this could propel me to greater heights - but it would be up to me to make things happen. This spurred me on and I played everywhere that would have me. When I wasn't playing, I was checking out other gigs, and when I wasn't checking out other gigs, I was buying records, and when I wasn't buying records . . . well, then I was playing - I was doing nothing else. Suddenly, from being a DJ, which is a solitary profession, I had colleagues. Look at me, sounding all business-like! These 'colleagues' were really just friends who were also playing records. Imagine replying when a careers teacher asks you what you want to do when you leave school: 'Play music to people dancing and having a good time'. They'd laugh in your face. But that was us. Even now, I smile when I think how high we had climbed in such a short time. A small group of us had pretty much single-handedly created a global industry that still thrives today and generates billions upon billions of dollars every year.

Could it get any better? Of course it could. We'd only just got started.

We were on the same bill as dance music pioneers like Frankie Knuckles, Juan Atkins, Marshall Jefferson and Kevin Saunderson. We all had a shared love of electronic music and the experimental sounds that had brought us to where we were. There had been a vibrant underground dance scene in the USA, especially in Detroit, Chicago and New York, which had seen the foundation of house and techno. The UK had had a very influential electronic pop scene with acts like Depeche Mode, Visage, Yazoo and the Human League. This had mixed with the Balearic sound from Alfredo's open-air Amnesia dancefloor in Ibiza, brought back to the UK by Danny Rampling, Nicky Holloway and Paul Oakenfold, and was injected with US house to give birth to acid house. You could walk into Paul's Spectrum and see Amnesiacs dancing alongside clubland legends like the Blitz's Rusty Egan, with bands like U2 and the Happy Mondays looking on. This scene went stratospheric very quickly; it made superstars of the US pioneers and made the UK the centre of the global dance music world. Suddenly, we were all discovering new music and new ways of playing it.

Pete Tong's *Essential Mix* show on BBC Radio 1 was and still is an important showcase for the multitude of genres and DJing styles that sit under the electronic music banner. It quickly became a bucket list thing for DJs to do, enabling the listeners to experience eclectic sounds from the likes of Pan-Pot, Moby, DJ Dmitry from Deee-Lite, Booka Shade, José Padilla, Howie B, Freddy Fresh, Andrew Weatherall, Chase & Status, Felix da Housecat and Bicep. Apparently, I hold the honour of the most *Essential Mixes* after Pete himself, with twenty-three shows across 1998 and 1999.

Human beings like to know where they come from. We seem obsessed with our family trees, what our ancestors did and how the things today came to be. It's the same with music. Everything has to come from somewhere, and I guess it's the way the human brain works - we like things neat and tidy. We need answers for everything. We were taught at school that Newton sat under a tree and an apple fell on his head and he discovered what we call gravity. Gravity must have been around before, but this dude rubbing his head is now a genius. Why? Because he sat under a tree and let an apple fall on him - some genius, huh!

The origins of electronic music should be easy to pinpoint because, as the name suggests, you need electricity to make it work. There were lots of pioneers plugging things in, making sounds and putting the building blocks in place for us. But I think if you ask anyone who the true pioneers of electronic music are, if you could only pick one, they will always say one word. Kraftwerk.

Just saying it sends shivers through me. Kraftwerk were formed in Germany in 1970 and continue to be the most influential electronic music pioneers who are still at the beating heart of techno today. It wasn't a band that you'd expect to see live in the 70s. There wasn't any 'show' in the normal sense of the word. There were four guys standing in a straight line with keyboards, drum machines and synthesisers in front of them, playing repetitive beats, repetitive melodies and the odd vocal, mostly through a vocoder. These geniuses gave us albums like *Autobahn*, *The Man-Machine* and *Trans-Europe Express*. Their influence is everywhere, from Bowie to hip-hop and from Daft Punk to Coldplay. These guys looked and behaved like robots. They were known to be odd, not in a diva sort of way, but in the way that their creativity was always switched on.

There's a famous story that the telephone in their studio did not have a ringer and they would answer calls at a set time, by appointment only. Apparently, Johnny Marr of the Smiths wanted to talk about a collaboration and was given a time to call so that the ringer wouldn't disrupt the creative process. He called exactly as requested and Ralph Hütter answered the phone with his trademark '*Ja*', even though the phone hadn't rung.

I knew I needed to meet these guys. I also knew that they needed to meet me, but they didn't know they needed to meet me and by didn't know, I mean didn't care and by didn't care, I mean they had no bloody idea who I was. But that was their problem. I felt that I had to get close to them. Maybe the magic would rub off on me. We'd all heard the rumours that Universe were trying to get them for Tribal Gathering '97 which was again going to be staged at Luton Hoo. As the line-up began to be confirmed, I could see this was going to be special. The Universe motto is 'eclectic electronic stimulation for the communication generation, lovingly provided for clubbers by clubbers', and they were going all out to deliver.

They started off by confirming live acts including Orbital, DJ Shadow, Juno Reactor, Faithless, Republica and Moloko. Like any festival, there is a process to bookings, and offers come in as they build their line-ups. Normally I'd sit back and watch my calendar fill up; as I'd been a big part of the Universe parties from the start, I knew they would book me. But as time went on and other acts were confirmed - Jeff, Richie, Laurent, Sasha, Sven and Paul, as well as Deep Dish and Masters at Work plus a couple of unusual bookings such as John Peel and James Lavelle - I couldn't wait any longer. I called them up to offer my services.

I didn't know that they'd actually booked me earlier that day and when I spoke to them on the phone, they were confused and during the chat let slip that Kraftwerk had just confirmed, but that I wasn't supposed to tell anyone. And I didn't . . . for at least thirty seconds, at which point I got on the blower to everyone: 'Kraftwerk is coming!'

I was going to try something new. I would play a stand-alone set to open the whole festival. I'd play outdoors on a specially built stage just before all the other arenas opened up. I would be the central planet at this Universe and unite all the different dance tribes across all genres. It turned into a really special set. I played to the entire festival audience in what became known as Carl's Morning Service: 'Dearly beloved, Let us play!' I feel like I played one of my most inspired and energetic sets as a tribute to Kraftwerk, who I'd seen arriving only a few hours earlier. The great thing about being an artist at a festival is that you have a special pass that allows you to wander around pretty much wherever you want. I was able to get close and catch the end of the epic 8½-hour support set from the Two Lone Swordsmen sound system featuring Andrew Weatherall and Keith Tinniswood before Kraftwerk came on for their first live performance anywhere in the world for years.

The original masters of machine music did not disappoint. Hearing their precision and craftsmanship made me realise why they are regarded as a primary influence by almost every producer of contemporary electronic dance music. It made me see how far we had come but also how far we could go. They filled my mind with ideas that even now I still use in the studio. It was a surreal moment because standing around me was DJ royalty, including the great Detroit DJs, who'd all closed their arena down as none of them wanted to miss this, all standing there in awe of the magic being created by Kraftwerk. It can't have been easy for them to be so adored by so many and looking at them you couldn't be sure if they weren't actually robots. They seemed so connected to their machines that at some points I couldn't work out if they were powering the machines or the machines were powering them. For sure, they were powering us!

With Kraftwerk at the forefront, Germany can lay claim to being the birthplace of the machine-made electronic music sound that has evolved into the various dance music genres we know and love. I'd been going to Germany since the early 1990s, when they'd embraced the acid house culture from the UK but decided that it needed to be harder and faster. I'd had some great experiences and played some awesome gigs, like when I played at Munich Airport in 1994. That was a mad one – thousands of party people at an event co-promoted from the UK where most people spoke little English – and my German is *nicht gut*. It wasn't long after the reunification of Germany so people really felt that the coming-together part of the scene was as important as the music.

Everyone wanted to hear and see what was going on and there were lots of film crews inside the event, which was an unusual thing as the UK raves had learned the hard way that letting loved-up clubbers loose in front of reporters was not necessarily a good thing. But in Munich it was different. The film crews saw this as a positive cultural thing and they needed someone who spoke English and who was a DJ to talk them through it. The promoters asked me if I'd mind. You joking? I'm trying to make a name for myself – of course I'll have some of that!

Suddenly people who had heard of me or seen me DJing could hear me talking. When I talk about music and parties I talk with passion, and this came through here, which suddenly made me a person beyond the name. I was offered more and more gigs and the opportunity to be part of special moments in the fledgling dance music world.

In 1997 I returned to the land of Kraftwerk to perform at the Love Parade. Berlin's Love Parade had started as an underground political demonstration that wanted to use music to foster peace and international understanding. It was started in July 1989 by Matthias Roeingh as his birthday party, and 150 people turned up. This was a few months before the collapse of the Berlin Wall as a barrier and two years before it was completely dismantled. Matthias, or Dr Motte as he is known, didn't have any big plans but the word spread and the annual event grew rapidly. By 1996 it had outgrown the streets it was on and the 1997 Love Parade moved to the Tiergarten, the park in the heart of Berlin that has a road leading straight from its centre to the iconic Brandenburg Gate. I was booked to play there and couldn't wait. I'd just seen Kraftwerk and now Dr Motte was bringing me to the greatest dance music stage in the world.

The 1997 Love Parade had over one million revellers at it – and I mean 'at it' in every sense of the phrase. The togetherness and freedom of partying in the open air in the middle of a city had made the Love Parade a bucket-list thing, even before bucket lists had become a thing. It was something that everyone needed to experience once, and that once seemed to happen the day I arrived to play.

Thinking about it, I reckon this was the day when the word 'play' would become replaced by 'perform' and the word 'gig' would be replaced by 'show'. And what a show it was. Dr Motte had pulled sound equipment and staging in from everywhere and with a million sets of feet and ears waiting on every beat you couldn't fail. I don't mean that you couldn't fail because it was like shooting fish in a barrel – I mean you couldn't *afford* to fail and let down the people who had come to dance. This wasn't just about *how* I played but *what* I played. I'd got three record boxes worth of tunes, some new and some old, hopefully more hits than misses, and I needed to tell a story for them and take everyone on a journey with me.

It felt like everything was leading to this. I'd been working my way up and had been involved with lots of magical moments – warming up for Danny Rampling on the opening night at Shoom, playing at Energy and Tribal Gathering, releasing my first track on Perfecto and performing it on *Top of the Pops* – but nothing prepares you for headlining in front of so many people. The equivalent of 48 Madison Square Gardens were stretched out in front of me, and all around me, and I was just standing there with a pile of records. Waiting to go up onto the platform seemed to take forever. I was feeling more nervous than usual and thinking that maybe they weren't ready for me or – even worse – that I wasn't ready for them. My mouth was dry and I kept trying to focus on what I needed to do, but it was impossible. Everything was a something. It was as if I could see the energy that seemed to magically transform the entire landscape and everyone in it. I was trying not to take it all in but at the same time I wanted to take it all in - maybe this was as good as it was going to get.

Most of the backstage people were German so I didn't really understand much of what they were saying, but I remember this guy working on the scaffolding and catching his eye. I remember thinking as he looked at me that it wasn't so long ago that I was also a scaffolder, and here I was about to do the thing I love the most in front of the biggest crowd ever assembled. Any nerves were gone, and Coxy was back in the room!

I hit the decks hard and played a blinder, if I say so myself. The enormity of the occasion wasn't lost on me and I made sure that I crafted my set to convey the respect I had for what Love Parade wanted to achieve. People were coming together and I wanted to be a part of that process. I could see the crowd - well, at least the few thousand nearest me - reacting well to the set and I kept digging deeper and deeper. I could have played forever, but time was drawing things to an inevitable close. I remember thinking about what to leave on and how I could make sure that I would leave them with something properly clever rather than too clever by half, while making the crowd think about the next chapter of our electronic music future. Looking back, it must have come to me suddenly, but thinking about it now I can rationalise it and say that we'd had a shared experience as we journeyed into the depths of house music and that was the reason for my final choice - creating that 'aha' moment. Whichever it was, I still to this day remain happy with my selection. I played the beginning of 'Rock Da House', the supremely catchy track by the Beatmasters featuring the Cookie Crew.

> 'I want to tell you all a story about House'
> *'House? What house?'*
> 'House music!'
> *'House Music?'*
> 'Yeah, you know . . . House!'

As I played this first a capella part I switched off the turntable so the phrase slowed down and came to a long drawn-out stop on the final 'House'. The perfect ending.

So that was the Berlin Love Parade, with one million people dancing to me as I stood in the shadow of the Brandenburg Gate. I really felt that I'd worked out what made a crowd tick and this set reinforced that. I was in the land of Kraftwerk and sharing my own take on electronic music. Amazingly, I was voted No. 1 DJ for the second year running in the *DJ Mag* Top 100 so I was front and centre with every festival and club promoter in the world. I'd been voted No.1 by the *DJ Mag* team in '96 but it was the public who went on to vote me No.1 in '97. People were listening to what I had to say on a scale that I could never have envisaged.

Success is a strange thing. Before you have it, you think that once you achieve your goals you're done, you can take it easy, but it's actually the opposite. Your goals change and while you still have the drive to succeed you need to work harder to get there.

Dance music has a way of joining the dots, and thirty years on from Dr Motte's legendary birthday party he is still celebrating. His birthday party in 2019 was at Berlin's Suicide Club and one of the artists performing was Saytek Live, a true electronic musician, whose tracks I play out and who has been signed to my Awesome Soundwave label. Saytek, (real name Joseph Keevill) plays live techno using cutting-edge digital technology alongside analogue synths, sequencers and drum machines. It's fitting that his next-level performances have been hosted by Dr Motte in Berlin.

Kraftwerk are really into modern techno, incorporating it into their new tracks, and it makes me smile to think that, in our own small way, we now influence the influencers. In June 2020 there was meant to be a Pioneers of Electronica event at Printworks in London that had lined up Visage's Rusty Egan, William Orbit and Saytek Live to play alongside former Kraftwerk 'Music Soldat' Wolfgang Flür. Despite the show being postponed, I've connected with Wolfgang and working with this icon is something that I could never have imagined happening.

So, wherever you're reading this, why not look up and say the word 'Kraftwerk' as we acknowledge the shoulders of the giants that we are standing on. Go on, you know you want to.

'Kraftwerk.'

9.

The White Isle

Ibiza wasn't always a place to party, famous for hedonism, super-clubs and DJ royalty. When I first went there it felt like I was going to the most exotic place ever, an island full of history that was easy to get to yet still only had a couple of hard roads. It was a place you could go to and call yourself a proper traveller.

One of the things most people crave is a nice summer holiday. There's something about the sun shining down on you that makes you happy. I was fed up with telling people 'nowhere' when they'd ask me where I'd been. I guess you're now expecting me to launch into a whole summer Ibiza vibe with me trying to get you to think that 'the kid did good, didn't he?' Actually, I want to start talking about summer vibes with a little story about vampires.

I'd been asked to bring my sound system to a summer party through friends of friends of friends. They specifically didn't want me to DJ, which was annoying because I'd just bought some great soul records that would be perfect for a summer's evening. When I got to the party, though, I could see why. I guess you'd call this lot goths. They were going to have an arm-flailing zombie-fest and just needed the sound equipment to play their music on. From the minute I walked in, I stood out like a sore thumb. Other than me, everyone else was white, dressed head to toe in black and looking very pasty. I asked one of the guys what this was all about and he said that everyone there was an individual and wanted to express their own identity. I looked at a room full of identical vampire types and it reminded me a bit of Monty Python's *Life of Brian*. 'We are all individuals!'

It made me want to giggle out loud but I managed to stop myself - didn't want my smile to ruin the vibe. They were actually a really nice bunch of people and I could see that they just wanted to have a good time.

It wasn't long before the clubbers from the emerging dance scene were being compared to vampires. Up all night and sleeping all day (in some cases, up all night and up all day and then up all night again!) - that's why the summer became such a big thing, because you could go out all night, especially in Europe where things seemed to go on until the early hours, and then collapse on a beach and spend the day soaking up the rays and chilling before doing it all over again.

One of the things that made Ibiza so magical and such a draw wasn't the nightlife, but the sun. When you think about it, a lot of what goes on revolves around the sun. There is the sunrise you see after dancing under the stars, there is the sunshine throughout the day and there are the magical sunsets. I'd been going to Ibiza since 1985, enjoying the island, listening to great DJs and having fun. In those days, of course, my fun was on the strictest budget. I had to really save up for any luxuries like a summer holiday and, like I mentioned earlier, in '87 I didn't have enough money to go on that legendary trip - who knows, it could have been the Ibiza Five!

My first trip to the island was done about as cheaply as you could. I rented a Fiat Panda and, after putting the seats down, my girlfriend, my sister and myself all slept in the car. We'd wake up with the sun burning us though the glass and head over to a hostel to wash and get ready for the day ahead.

For my first few visits to Ibiza, I was firmly rooted in San Antonio. It was all I could afford. Everything I did had to be super-cheap so I took in some of the rustic sights and did what all lads do, which was save up for the clubs and parties that were advertised on the flyers being handed out on the beach. I wasn't very adventurous at that point and, being a bit unsure of the local cuisine, stuck mainly to spaghetti bolognaise with fries or - if I was pushing the boat out - a party bucket of Kentucky.

Often I'd be sharing an apartment with a bunch of mates and as a treat we'd hire mopeds to whizz around on. One night, we stumbled across an after-hours party just off the main drag to Ibiza town that had been organised by Tommy Mac, a dancer from London, who was a whirlwind of what I can only describe as partying craziness. I remember thinking that the crowd looked very sophisticated and that everyone was having a great time. Me and my mates thought we'd up our game and order a cocktail bowl called the 'Coco-Loco', a bit like a fancy pina colada. Turns out, this one had an added ingredient - a healthy dose of MDMA - and it wasn't long before I could see why everyone was having such a good time. I don't remember much about that party but I do remember the long walk back the next day from the apartment to collect the moped that I'd left outside.

I went to Ibiza just to go and listen to other DJs. I never actually played there until about 1990/91. A guy called Mensa who used to run a club called Sterns in Worthing, West Sussex, was the South Coast promoter who really made a difference to the scene. He decided he wanted to go to Ibiza and take the Sterns DJs with him. I was one of them and he wanted me to be a part of it. The club we went to is now called Eden, but before that it was called Kaos and before that the Star Club. I also played another one for him on San Antonio bay, and one near Pacha as well. I played all these clubs and rocked the shit out of them! Then people on the island were like: 'Who is this DJ?' That's how I got to play in Ibiza.

Once the Summer of Love was underway, and due to my growing popularity in the UK, I started to get some nice bookings in Ibiza. I played everywhere that would have me and got to see some of the great DJs like Alfredo at Pacha. It was at the Star Club where I made my name. Clockwork Orange were next door and, although we weren't in competition, they had really locked into the Ibiza party ethos. I'd already decided that I would be focusing on the music. I love having fun but when it comes to my music, I always remember why I'm there. I would always play and then go straight back home, be it to a villa, apartment, hotel or straight back to the UK. Obviously, as my name grew and I started to play later and later, I would never get home before the sun was up, but my policy was always the same: play, then home. I remember one night where I was at Summum and had stayed on because I was on the earliest flight back to the UK, I had a bit of a cold and it seemed a good idea to drink vodka and orange - for the Vitamin C, of course. By the time I finished at 6am and headed to the airport, I'd had so much to drink that I struggled at the check-in desk. With a little bit of time to kill, I thought I'd better eat something to level me up and went for a grilled cheese sandwich. I have a very strong constitution, but I reckon the poison of the alcohol began attacking the grease of the cheese, and I started to turn green. I was pouring with sweat and reached the point of no return. I made it to the bathroom with a record box in each hand, kicked the cubicle door open and luckily there was no one in there. I was so sick, it was like something out of *Alien*. It was all up the back wall and everywhere in between. I made a half-hearted attempt to clean it up as best I could before heading to the flight. I managed to keep it together all the way back to the UK, but the poor lady sitting next to me looked terrified at this big, sweating guy moaning all the way there with a large sick bag open on my lap. Lesson learned.

The great thing about the sun is that it shines everywhere and makes people, especially young people, want to have fun. I was already playing in other countries and building my name to ever-growing audiences who were then heading back home. Not just to the UK, but to Germany, France, Italy, the Netherlands and further afield. One club that sticks in my mind was BCM in Mallorca. The manager at BCM, Tony Palmer, loved the UK rave scene and went out of his way to book the best DJs for the club. I had some great times there and the crowd were always really up for a good party.

I've always prided myself on my interaction with my fans. In fact, I don't think of them as 'fans' but as people who have a shared interest in music; every time someone comes up to me, I always reach out to them because I know they are coming to me because my music has connected with them. It is very important for all of us in the industry to remember why we are able to do what we do. It is the people who listen to our music and fill out dancefloors that are the special ones, because without them we couldn't exist.

Most fans mean well but sometimes they get a little carried away and don't quite think through what they say or do. One time I was playing at BCM and I was just getting my records out of the car on a very warm Mallorcan evening when this guy came running over to me. One of the security guys tried to hold him back and told him that he could catch me in the club, but I could see he couldn't wait and he looked like he was about to explode, so I waved him through. He came up to me and told me that I was his second-favourite DJ in the whole world! He was absolutely bloody serious. It didn't occur to him to lie and say I was his favourite. I asked him who his favourite was, and he looked at me as if I was crazy and said, 'Paul Oakenfold, of course.' Hopefully, I rocked him enough in the set later on to at least keep my number-two position!

I remember one time when Tony booked me to play for 5,000 people and things did not go as planned. The club finished quite early: the lights would go on at 3am. He'd booked me to play but, because of other commitments, I could only arrive that night, which was cool as I was used to just getting off a plane and being ready to rock and roll. I'd done this with Tony before as well, so he wasn't particularly worried and had a sell-out crowd ready and waiting for me. It was a pretty standard thing and as the plane flew over Mallorca, I was ready to shake that dancefloor to its foundations. At least I would have been, had we landed! The plane began its descent, seatbelts were on, tables were up, then as we came right above the runway, the plane went straight back up in the air and flew off. They announced it was too windy in Mallorca to land, so we were heading to Barcelona! As soon as we landed, I phoned Tony. He went absolutely crazy with me. He was standing at the airport in Mallorca, where he said there was no wind and planes were landing all over the place. The only plane that wasn't landing was the one he was waiting for that had me on it, ready to be taken to the club to entertain 5,000 people – who would be after a full refund at the very least.

I didn't want to disappoint Tony and I sure as hell didn't want to disappoint the clubbers. I was talking to the check-in desk and they were trying to decide whether to put us all up in hotels in Barcelona and fly us the next day or whether they would fly us back straight away; I think the cost of the hotels meant that they decided to get rid of us and fling us back to Mallorca. By midnight I was back on the plane and at 1.30am Tony was dragging me from the airport into his car to get me to the club.

Remember, the club closes at 3am, so Tony drove in a way that would have impressed a seventeen-year-old Carl Cox. I spent that journey trying to focus on what I had to do at the club while concentrating on staying alive, which basically involved telling Tony to keep his eyes on the road because every time he spoke/yelled at me, he would look directly at me. We made it, but I had to throw down two or three tequilas as I got into the DJ booth, mainly to steady myself from that car journey. The clubbers had no idea of what had happened, and I came on and absolutely smashed it. My set was long enough for everyone to be happy, especially me, and when I went over to Tony at the end of the night, he looked as if nothing had happened and it was just all in a day's work.

All these summer adventures were great. I was having the time of my life, playing the music I wanted to an appreciative audience and seeing the dance music community grow and grow. What I didn't know was that just around the corner would be a meeting with an Ibizan local, past the age of retirement, who would see something in me; and together we would redefine Ibizan nightlife.

I was playing everywhere. I had played at Pacha, Privilege, Amnesia and Summum when Pepe Rosello and Fritz Pangratz convinced me that their club, Space, could be for me. We spoke long into the night and realised that we could make this different to all the other clubs. They weren't worried about big line-ups but were really focused on the music and the experience of the people that came. We also decided that we would open early – we would get going at 10pm, which is earlier than all the other clubs.

In 1996 I'd been invited to Space by React for the album-release party for *At the End of the Cliché* and that's where I met Pepe. Pepe had taken a lease on the land and had created a club. He is a wonderful man, incredibly considerate, the best host, and just knows how to treat people really well. We really connected and he felt the energy in my music and how I played it. So I started my regular night there. Pepe and I imagined that it might run for four summer seasons. The thing is, that would probably have been the case if it had started with a bang and then tailed off, like most clubs, where it's hard to sustain the original dream. Clubbers evolve and are always looking for the next big thing. But not only did we start with a bang and create the next big thing, by evolving we also unwittingly became the next big thing after that. My whole adventure at Space from day one was promoted by Lynn Cosgrave and Safehouse, alongside Eoin Smyth and Dave Browning, who turned promoting in Ibiza into an art form. There were lots of different names for the night: 'Carl Cox and Friends' became 'Carl Cox Revolution', but really it was Carl Cox at Space. We started in 2001 and this residency ran without a break until

2016 and when it ended, it was on the highest note possible. It never tailed off and never went down. The clubbing experience and the music we provided continued to soar and could easily still be growing to this day. Nothing was broken. In the end, it was all about business. Pepe's deal with the family who owned the land had come to an end after twenty-seven years and, although he was supposed to be able to renew it, they didn't want it to happen.

By now, Pepe was eighty-three and had achieved so much that we decided not to fight it. I have a few plans up my sleeve for me and Ibiza but in the meantime I enjoy nothing more than being over at his place on the island for dinner. Pepe is a great cook - no spag bol for me here, but delicious local recipes made with love. He also likes opera and bursts into song at every opportunity. He'd always sing happy birthday to me over the microphone at Space on my big day.

Ibiza, which actually has a very small population, made its name as a hippy traveller destination and, like all the Balearic islands, became a tourist hot spot. Every tourist place has its USP - unique selling point. With Ibiza, it became the island of music. Some of the great DJs who'd spread dance music all around the world took with them some of the Ibiza spirit that they picked up from visiting the island. I've heard so many great DJs play there and the ones that really stand out in my mind as I write this, who embody the Ibizan spirit, include Cesar, Alfredo, Pippi, David Morales, Simon Dunmore and Clara Da Costa. You can learn a lot from watching and listening to someone doing what they love with such passion. There are so many great tracks that I first heard in Ibiza or that were influenced by Ibiza that bring back amazing memories. Every season would have two or three standout tunes and you knew when you first played them that within two or three months they would be played all over the world. Some would stand the test of time while others were just for the moment, but all of them helped shape the mood on the island. I still play many of these tracks in my sets and with my virtual shows like *Cabin Fever* I can read the online comments, which often include people saying, 'I remember when I first heard you play that track at Space!'

At the same time, while I was playing, people were handing me white labels and their own creations to listen to, and there were clearly some great things happening not just in recording studios but being made in people's bedrooms. Dance music and technology went hand in hand and someone could make a track in their bedroom, press up a couple of white labels on the cheap, get them into a DJ's hand and have it played to a big club audience – and this could all happen within a week.

There are two standout records for me that capture the spirit of Ibiza. One is Paul Oakenfold's 'Jibaro', which was a reworking of the Elkin & Nelson Latin dancefloor filler that he'd first heard played by Alfredo, and the other is Joe Smooth's 'Promised Land', which is about as timeless as can be.

As I got more into the whole Ibizan vibe, I also started to go to other clubs and parties. As the awareness of who I was grew, it became harder for me to actually enjoy myself on the dancefloor – everyone assumes that you want to talk about other projects when actually all you want to do is have a good time. One big exception to this was Manumission. Mike and Claire McKay had created a super-club, which was basically a playground for grown-ups without any boundaries where interesting music and interesting people collided. It was a bit like the freedom that used to exist in Ibiza on the open-air dancefloor at Amnesia, and their night would also include their after-hours carry-on parties, which were even wilder than the club night. I was there on that now infamous night in 1994 when they opened the Manumission Motel in a rundown ex-brothel on the wrong side of town. A whole load of us were there for the opening night including Pete Tong, Fatboy Slim and Danny Rampling, alongside a diverse bunch of Mike and Claire's friends including Kate Moss, Primal Scream, Howard Marks and even Roman Polanski.

Mike and Claire pushed the party hard. It turned into a 36-hour frenzy that has since been given various names, like The Lost Weekend and 'That Night'. It was absolutely mad. They basically opened the Motel as a place for themselves, their DJs, a bunch of strippers who they'd befriended and all their mates to hang out. The thing is, in Ibiza, everyone is your mate. So, this place was absolutely heaving. I remember that I was in Room 14 and there was no hot water. I tried to complain to Johnny, who was on the door, but I think my hot-water problems were the least of his worries. By this point, I was only wearing a toga and a pink wig and I definitely broke my rule of leaving at a sensible time. This was one of the most epic nights of all time and a sensory overload. The crazy thing was, this was actually only the start of my longest sesh ever! By Monday, and still going strong, I had to get on a plane to fly to Mallorca to DJ and had to go all the way through until the next morning, when I got straight on another plane to Portugal, where I played another mega-set, before getting back to Ibiza on Wednesday late afternoon and collapsing into bed, having been 'on the go' since Saturday. Amazingly, when I surfaced on the Thursday and walked out into the sunshine, the first people I saw were coming back from the opening night of the Motel, four days earlier!

*

During the season in Ibiza, everything is fun. As the scene has grown there seem to be activities that go on all day long to add to that Balearic experience. You see clubbers up to all sorts of mischief during the day and you've got to wonder how they've got the strength to do that all day and night throughout their holiday.

I've also done things that are not quite in my comfort zone. I got involved in this 'DJ Cook Off', which seemed like a good idea at the time and was basically some sort of cooking competition for DJs judged by people who knew about food. But what seems like a good idea on paper isn't necessarily a good idea when you're out in the field. Clearly none of us had the time to devote to this so we all came up with our own way of making sure that we would triumph. I was sure I was gonna win with my incredible minestrone bean soup, which tastes like the sort of dish you get in a five-star London restaurant. The reason for this is that you really could get it in a five-star London restaurant! My friend Andy Needham, *chef patron* at L'Amarosa, made this incredible soup that helped him win his Michelin award. I loved it so he made me a batch, froze it and sent it out to me in Ibiza, where I defrosted it, plated it up beautifully and topped it off with a couple of langoustines. The soup was so good that I felt I couldn't lose, which is why I was so hacked off when I didn't win. Top honours went to DJ and producer Kölsch. To be fair to the guy, he had arranged for a whole pig to be flown in from Finland that had been lovingly prepared for him by *his* favourite Michelin-star chef.

Ibiza really has the power to make things happen for you; there must be hundreds of thousands of people who are turned on to great music without even realising it. Most of the time, everything is about being happy and smiling and connecting with people. But Ibiza has a way of taking hold of your feelings and giving you experiences that you weren't expecting and bringing out some of the best qualities of your own personality. All this is done through amazing nights and the power of music. That's what keeps drawing me back to Ibiza.

I like people to say hello while I'm playing and I like a bit of atmosphere with people dancing around me, but I also know that I'm there for the crowd. I don't want things to get so busy on stage that people feel that's where the real party is. There has been an extraordinary collection of people who've been to my Ibizan nights while I'm playing and have stopped by to shake hands. P. Diddy hung out at the DJ booth at Space, and one night Dr Dre came in - I was like, WTF? He could see I was stunned and said, 'Just keep doing your thing. I love it.'

I normally stay at Pepe's villa when I'm there; he mainly lives in an apartment in town. Despite the fact that I spend so much time in Ibiza, I've never wanted to buy a house there. It's strange, but I don't think I would enjoy owning a place there - even though I really feel like Ibiza is a second home to me. When I go there, and from the moment the plane lands, I feel I am in a special place. I don't get that feeling anywhere else in the world. Having my own place there would add a layer of responsibility that I worry would eat into the freedom I feel when I get there. I've never treated Ibiza in any way other than as an amazing place to be. I love the people and the pace of the island and I am very lucky that I've been able to share this with others.

Part of that experience was that all the DJs playing with me at Space would stay at the villa. We'd hang out together, eat together and connect as a family. We'd head over to the club as a group and that bond was one of the main reasons that made that club night so special and successful. Pepe would come over and share his amazing stories about the early days in Ibiza and his special insights into people. He is unique - if you didn't have him you wouldn't have had Space. He always says that when you leave a club and the lights have come on the music remains behind, almost like it's stuck to the walls. Like the people who visit Graceland or walk over the zebra crossing outside Abbey Road Studios, people are drawn to the spot where hundreds of thousands of people danced and made memories on the dancefloor.

In 2019 a video went viral (thanks, *DJ Mag*!) of me stopping the music at a club in Greece because some people were fighting. A lot was made of this, but it was just one of those things. What a lot of people don't know is that this has happened before. In 2010 there was a fight between two guys at the back of the dancefloor at Space. I watch a crowd very closely; you need to, during a set. And I could see these two guys going for each other. At first I thought it was nothing but then I could see it might escalate. You've got to remember that Space was my home away from home. I pulled the volume of the music right down, grabbed the mic and said: 'You in the black!' This wasn't a great choice of words, actually, as a lot of people were wearing black. A circle had formed around the guys and people were moving away. The crowd started to realise something was up and the security guys were moving towards them. They grabbed them just as I shouted out: 'NOT IN MY HOUSE!' A huge cheer went up from the crowd and I remember saying, 'Let's enjoy the music, people,' as we got straight back into it.

One of the most emotional nights was the last night at Space in 2016. We knew that this was it. For me, Space was one of the defining moments in my life history. I knew I'd been sharing my vision based on what I believed in and that this was now going to stop and, unlike most things in my life, I had no control over it. It was absolutely heartbreaking. We never really believed it would last four years, let alone fifteen years, but it just continued to get better and better and better. It got to the point where it was impossible to go to Ibiza and not see Carl Cox on a Tuesday.

Pepe wasn't going to let us go quietly. He had a full orchestra and choir singing, all wearing white, and we all wore white too. All of us on the stage had big smiles and I played a special mix of Frankie Knuckles's 'Your Love'. There were actually two closing sets that night. This part of it, with the choir, was in the main club and I played a nine-hour set. That sounds long, but the time flew past, with people coming up on the stage to give me a hug and share in the moment. I was also joined by good friends like Nic Fanciulli for B2B sets. Part two was inside in the discotheque. The emotions were really flying now. We'd had a spectacular run and attracted some awesome people and artists over the years, like Slash from Guns N' Roses and Madonna. But while I was standing there playing and looking at the crowd in front of me, I knew that it was the people that had made Space what it was. Without realising it, they had supported me all the way through. And it wasn't just me teaching them about my music; they were teaching me and making me push myself harder and further than I would have done without them. My final, final record of the night was Angie Stone's 'Wish I Didn't Miss You' and I'm not ashamed to say that the tears were streaming down my face.

We always had the opening fiesta of the summer at Space, which felt like the start of the season for the whole island. With Pepe as the host with the most we'd be joined by people from all over Ibiza as a celebration of what was to come. From there things would build up nicely across all the clubs and bars. Without that launching pad now it feels like something is missing. The whole new VIP culture and tables with high minimum spends means that some of the best parts of being in Ibiza, like hanging out and meeting random people, doesn't happen as much. Seeing empty tables reserved and waiting for the 'big spenders' takes away from the atmosphere of inclusivity. Having proper clubbers being overlooked by rich folks who are probably spending more that night than most people spend on their whole holiday creates an unnecessary divide.

Table versus dancefloor. We would never have had this as a focal point at Space and playing at other clubs now shows me why this doesn't work and can't possibly last. From where I stand, I can see who's really having the better time.

Life has a way of throwing things up when you least expect it - who'd have thought when I was having my first lads' holiday in Ibiza that I would go on to help create one of the best clubs in our lifetime and one that still resonates all across the world. For a small island, Ibiza has a big heart, and it has touched a lot of hearts and souls from all over the world. 2020 was a very tough year on the island and I felt sad to see how quickly the islanders started to suffer with all the clubs closed. In November I played a virtual show from Melbourne to help raise funds and awareness for the Ibiza Food Bank, which is supporting families, many of whom are reliant on the money that tourism brings in.

The level of quality we delivered at Space might be equalled some day, and I hope it will be. But I do not believe the magic we created at Space will ever be bettered. I'm sure there will be experiences that come close and that the specialness will be equalled but, as for bettered, when it comes to the magic, we already created the best of the best.

10.

Back to the Future

The year 2000 was coming. There was a lot of hype about the millennium and, like everyone else, I was excited. There was no reason to be, really, it was just another year, but it seemed like a new beginning for everyone. As 1999 progressed and Prince was hopefully enjoying the bonus royalties from the huge amount of radio play he was getting, we started to hear about the dreaded Y2K computer bug. This wasn't some sort of creature that would hatch out of your PC and take over the world, but a possible problem because of the way only two digits had been used to program the date in most computers – so '99' would be followed by '00'. We would literally enter year zero. This would mean that everything would reset itself and scientists in white coats were popping up all over the news telling us that in a worst-case scenario nuclear bombs could launch themselves and planes would fall out of the sky. So where did I decide to be on New Year's Eve? Yep, on a plane.

In the dance music world, New Year's Eve would be another big party. But because it was the millennium, people were charging huge amounts of money for tickets and some artists were charging ridiculous fees. I didn't really understand that, because if it was going to be the end of the world, where would they spend it?

My plan was that I would see in the new millennium – by definition a once-in-a-lifetime experience – twice! I'd DJ for the New Year's Eve countdown in Australia, then race to the airport and fly halfway around the world to Hawaii, beating the international time zones to then be able to DJ at midnight in Honolulu. The idea had come to Eddie Gordon, who was working with Pete Tong and wanted to use this to showcase BBC Radio 1's worldwide commitment to dance music by doing something no one had ever done before. At this point, a lot of my arrangements were sorted out by Rachel Birchwood, who I guess you could call my executive PA, and it just so happened that Rachel was with Eddie and was actually heavily pregnant and about to have her first child. (I was actually amazed when recently, their daughter Olivia, now all grown up, turned up in Ibiza on my guest list.)

Anyway, back to New Year's Eve. My first gig was actually in the open air on Bondi Beach, run by the guys behind Cream. It was very windy and, being an all-vinyl show back then, the needles started jumping across the turntables. Playing before me were Eric Powell and Ralph Lawson, and they were having real problems with the weather. A carpenter was called up in the middle of the show to build a windbreak around the DJ booth and by the time I got there the turntables were protected from the elements and the show was great, an amazing New Year's Eve midnight countdown as we entered the new millennium and the year 2000.

When it was midnight in Australia it was lunchtime in the UK and Radio 1 went live. It was a totally new concept and it was great that the BBC were behind it as they had the skills to make sure the sound was really good. Looking back on it now, I can say that this show was the template for the streaming that would take place in the future and that is now a common part of the dance music scene. We proved that you can be there without actually being there.

So this was the big one. Fireworks were going off, everyone was cheering, kissing, hugging and celebrating the dawn of a new era. I think that subconsciously everyone had a quick glance in the sky to see if any planes or astronauts were crashing down, but obviously the scientists at Nerdsville HQ had worried us for nothing. Then again, maybe the hundreds of billions of dollars spent worldwide to fix the problem had something to do with it.

I played until 4am on Bondi Beach and then got ready to travel over 5,000 miles to Hawaii. Originally, Michael Jackson was going to do the two-time-zone party with shows in Australia and Hawaii, but his people had advised him that it wasn't safe to fly that night. My thinking was that if Qantas were happy to send a plane up in the air then it must be safe. It was one of the best decisions I ever made and helped show the world that clubland had come of age. I had soaked in the atmosphere of 2000 for a few hours and realised that it wasn't that different to 1999. Time to make doubly sure. It was time to go time-travelling.

We headed over to the airport to get on the flight to Hawaii and, I must say, I was a little bit nervous because I still thought there was a slim chance that something might go wrong. Anyway, without stretching out the drama, we arrived in Hawaii. We'd crossed the international date line and here I was back on 31 December 1999.

I was playing on the Kakaako Waterfront Beach in Honolulu at a free event that really put Hawaii on the map for dance music. The reception I received was amazing. Not only was this the biggest dance music event ever to hit the island, but it was also endorsed by the Governor of Hawaii as the official State of Hawaii millennium party. The party was called Future Hawaii 2000 and I had a track out called 'Phuture 2000', which was a perfect fit for them and became the anthem for the celebrations. I don't even know if they knew I'd made it but when I played it the party just went off. It was an incredible feeling to celebrate in this way. What I hadn't thought about was the wider audience who would be staying at home and listening to the broadcast. Radio 1 did their magic and my sets from both locations went live to millions. With all the anti-climax that you often get on New Year's Eve, which seemed intensified because of the expectation for the millennium, for people to be able to enjoy what I was doing for free and from the comfort of their own homes, surrounded by mates, felt the perfect way for me to give back for all the love that I had experienced that decade.

One of my best New Year's Eves was hosted by my good friend Lincoln Cheng at his Zouk club in Singapore. The club always looks spectacular, with amazing artwork like original Andy Warhols on the walls. It's a smallish club, perfect for creating a really intimate setting for the party. What stood out for me that night was a couple that came over and tried to talk to me in what I imagine was Mandarin. I didn't really have a clue about what they were saying but they had big smiles and gave me the universally recognised double thumbs-up. We basically connected through the music.

That trip to Hawaii was really special for me. I could have played anywhere, but I made the perfect choice. It really excited me to not only have to focus on delivering the ultimate sound but also having the challenge of getting to Hawaii on the night when everything was meant to fall apart - it really pushed me mentally and physically. I feel like I left my mark on the island and it is still one of the things that people talk to me about the most.

Twenty years later, I was still getting amazing offers for New Year's Eve. It's a great night to play and there are some fantastic events with excellent promoters who deliver value and fun on a night that people really want to enjoy. NYE is not just a party; for many people, they see it as a time to turn things around, the beginning of a new year, a new start, filled with high hopes of love, life and laughter. Then it came to me. On New Year's Eve 2019 I should go back to Hawaii. Forget the mega offers, this would be the perfect time to show the island how grateful I still am to them for taking me to their hearts and allowing me to celebrate with them. Electronic music hasn't really taken a hold in Hawaii so the place is mostly overlooked by American and international artists, which is a shame. It shouldn't be seen just as a place to do a gig, but a place to enjoy the natural beauty.

It wasn't as easy to organise this as I thought it would be, and we did it relatively last-minute. A chance meeting in London about a charity project between my manager and two West Coast promoters, Rafi and Steve, led to us putting a plan together for an NYE party in Honolulu so that I could welcome in 2020 as I had in 2000. The first hurdle was that Hawaii isn't keen on open-air events any more, especially near their beautiful beaches. I can understand this because, for some reason, no matter how respectful you are as a crowd, there still seems to be a human instinct to discard garbage; and leaving Hawaii with a mess of plastic bottles floating around would be the opposite of what I'd want to achieve. It's a bit like the big festivals where everybody says they support the environment, yet they leave their tents and rubbish behind and most of these things can only end up in landfill. Every festival should adopt the Burning Man approach.

We had to get creative. The first step was to secure a venue and we booked Republik, which has an awesome sound system. One of the most important things I felt I needed in order to go back was to connect to the open air, and I'm sure that we could have secured a licence if we'd had more time, but doing this ourselves from thousands of miles away and with no sponsors meant we had to think outside the box. In the end, the plan evolved. I would do New Year's Eve at Republik and the following day – New Year's Day – would perform in the open air to a small crowd, ideally on a boat as the sun set, so that I could truly have seen in 2020. Things started to come together and, in keeping with my vision, I opted for a wooden pirate galleon rather than your typical booze-cruise party boat. Eric Powell, who was part of my original millennium show, would fly out to support me, and Mark Lewis, aka Mark London, would fly in from LA. We would also be backed up by some local DJs.

We promoted it in a very low-key way, but even still, the sunset cruise sold out in less than sixty seconds. I had friends flying in from all over the place and I was looking forward to having a few days' break in Hawaii around the show. Of course, things are never that easy and it was time for Mr Curveball to rear his head again.

My mother had died a few years earlier and my father had been unwell for a long time with Alzheimer's and didn't really know what was going on, but he had taken a turn for the worse and, by mid-December 2019, I was told I'd better get out to Barbados as this could be it. I took a flight to LA, changed to Miami and then flew on to Bridgetown. My father was looking small and weak and obviously didn't really know where he was or even who I was, but it felt great to be with him.

My father didn't get behind my career much, even though I had him to thank for my first taste of great music. When I told him I wanted to be a DJ he actually laughed. I get it, he'd struggled on the buses and probably felt that I was looking for an easy route. I don't think he could see how I could support myself through music.

As my career propelled me to greater heights he could finally see that not only was I a success as a DJ but that I was at the front of something big and was internationally recognised for what I had started doing in his front room as a small boy. He only acknowledged my success in a way that was as if Carl Cox the DJ was a different person to Carl Cox his son. I felt what a shame it was that he never felt able to tell me he was proud of me; his dementia robbed me of the chance of recognition from the guy who had got me hooked on music in the first place.

We've lived apart, on opposite sides of the world, for many years, but he is my dad and, standing with him, I still felt like I was little Carl in the front room in Carshalton listening to those soul records on his prized record player. It was very difficult, thinking about next steps and potential funeral plans, and after a couple of days I headed back to LA, where I'd be based so that I could get to Barbados or Hawaii as needed.

Amazingly, my father improved, so I felt it was time to get back to Hawaii and start focusing on the show. Aloha again!

I'd brought my favourite Hawaiian shirts with me because, after all, when in Hawaii . . .! Two days before NYE, the opportunity came up for another gig as part of the Hawaiian experience, one that would take place at night on New Year's Day going through until 2 January. We got hold of a venue called The Penthouse, which was on the forty-first floor of a tower block and has 360-degree views around Honolulu. We decided to go for it and announced it, so now I had three shows to do, all totally different in character and size. I was excited.

The Republik show was great and I had decided to try to really connect with the audience on a personal level at midnight. It's a special moment for all of them but it was also special for me. I didn't have any balloon drops, confetti cannons or party hats, and I counted down to the new year myself on my trusty microphone. Oh yes, oh yes! It wasn't a massively late night but very emotional, and a whole bunch of us went back to the villa that we'd rented and hung out as we now officially joined the rest of the world in 2020.

The next day we headed down to the pirate galleon, which really looked like something straight out of the adventures of Captain Kidd – you could almost imagine the swashbucklers sword-fighting all over the place. This was a very intimate set. Health and safety meant fewer than a hundred people were allowed on the boat, including the crew. With no pressure and a pretty captive audience, we set sail and I played a set that I feel captured the moment. Somebody had a pirate hat with them and it ended up on my head. For most of the journey out to sea and back again, we were followed by several party boats, crammed to capacity but not playing any music. They were basically gate-crashing, or maybe I should say sea-crashing, our party. I'm cool with that and hope that whoever they were, they enjoyed themselves. Every sunset is magical, whether you're at Café del Mar in Ibiza or standing in your local park, but it felt good to have achieved this in Hawaii. Of course, when the sun goes down, it gets bloody cold, and we headed back so I could prepare for the party that night.

The Penthouse gig suddenly became complicated because it's a largely residential building with luxury apartments, and the word had spread that we were doing this party up on their roof. To fit in with the plans, we had to start on 1 January and to make sure that we stuck to these guidelines, the party kicked off at 11.45pm. I was back at the villa having decided to play myself from 4am until 8am, when I would close the party. Our promoters on the ground knew that I like excellent sound quality and had pushed the boat out to make sure everything was in place. And, had this been a typical nightclub, I'm sure everything would have been fine.

Unfortunately, with the party goers having to be brought up and down in lifts and congregating around the building and the extended music hours, this was never going to be popular with the residents – but we were just doing what the venue were happy for us to do. At about 2am, I got a call at the villa from Eric, who was at the venue and playing, to say that he'd been asked to lower the volume and he just thought I'd like to know that. No disrespect, Eric, if you're reading this, but that literally went in one ear and out the other. At 2.30am, Eric called me again to tell me the police had turned up, having had complaints about the noise. Now, I am an old-school promoter and I could see where this would be heading, so wasn't surprised when Eric phoned me at 3am, while I was on my way to the club, to tell me not to come down as the police were there again.

Well, I hadn't flown thousands of miles to not turn up to my own party, and it wasn't long before I was making my way up in the lift to the forty-first floor. I got in, stood behind the decks and got to work. I worked hard, making sure that the bass and treble were at the right level so people could enjoy the music but that it wouldn't be thudding too much to the floors below. A couple more visits from the police later and I could see that we wouldn't make 8am, so I knew I had to work away for the set to end on a good note, leaving everyone happy. Just after 6.30am, I felt I couldn't lower the sound any further and still deliver my musical vision, so brought the night to a close. A big round of applause from the crowd and smiles all round showed me that this Hawaiian experience had worked out perfectly.

I was exhausted and as I made my way down in the lift, I was thinking to myself that as a kid, I used to watch *Hawaii Five-o* and now here I was, as a grown-up, having my party stopped by the Honolulu police. This was a very different experience to the millennium and I enjoyed it in a different way. I'd had an amazing 2019. In one week alone I played sold-out shows in Ibiza, Athens, Brighton and Istanbul, plus a surprise B2B set with Fatboy Slim in London. On top of that I was named International DJ of 2019 at the DJ Awards. It felt very important for me to be in Hawaii after the incredible year that I'd just had and the amazing plans ahead; it was the perfect place to spend a few days chilling and recharging the batteries. It really is a paradise there and it's amazing to think that Hawaii is part of the USA. There's a different mentality on the islands and I vow not to leave it so long until my next visit. Hopefully, I left a little piece of me behind because I know that I took a little bit of Hawaii away in my heart.

I was now all set for the year to come. Like all of us, I had no idea just how challenging 2020 was going to be.

11.

Down Under

When I was growing up, a foreign holiday seemed exotic. Australia, the land of surfing, *Crocodile Dundee* and *Mad Max*, seemed like another planet. It was about as far away as you could ever get from England. I could never have imagined that I would end up setting up a home, building a studio and spending five months of the year based out in Melbourne.

Australia has been really good to me. I've built a big studio out there on my farm, Carl Cox Motorsport is based out there, it's where I launched the Mobile Disco and Pure festivals, and the place that has welcomed me with open arms. From my first trip to Australia, when I went to DJ, I thought this could be a place to settle down. I spend a lot of time based in the UK at my house in Hove, from where I travel throughout Europe and to the States, plus a lot of back and forths to Ibiza. While I think of that place as home, the nature of what I do means that I don't get much chance to make it *homely*.

Australia is different. I have so much going on over there that it has become my new first home. I love the weather, which is what attracted me to Australia in the first place, and I love the people, who are down-to-earth and friendly. I've been really lucky that my tour manager, Ian, also likes nice weather and the Aussie way of life and so has relocated out there, which means we don't waste time meeting up at random airports but can get going from the kick-off.

The Australian way of life is really laid-back, which suits me down to the ground. They love good food and company over there, both of which I like in abundance, and I've made some great friends, mostly not involved in dance music. Having the studio out there is so much more productive. You don't get random mates ringing the doorbell at all hours of the day and night, and the distractions of the 24/7 London party scene are not as accessible. If you want distractions, you have to go looking for them or make them up yourself.

I made my first trip to Australia in 1991. I was a known DJ on the UK rave scene but a promoter would have to be really confident that I could pull a crowd to fly me out. The thing that got me to Australia was being on *Top of the Pops* in the UK. My track, 'I Want You (Forever)' had crossed over on Australian radio and was being played at parties, so a couple of promoters decided to bring me out. You've got to remember that, up until this point, I hadn't been abroad much; suddenly, I was packed into an economy-class seat, heading to the land down under. It was wintertime, so I turned up wearing a thick, warm jacket with all my winter woollens. For Australia, it's all upside down – literally. Our winter is their summer. So here I was in this lovely, gorgeous weather while all my mates were shivering back home.

The promoters, Malcolm and Michelle, had arranged gigs for me in Sydney and Melbourne. Sydney was great but quite touristy, while Melbourne was just lovely. I instantly fell in love with the place and decided I wanted to go back there every year. And I have done. At the same time, the Australian dance scene started to take off and I was booked on the Big

Day Out festival, which gave me a reason to go back. I was going every year, doing my gigs and shows and then staying on for a bit. It was starting to cost me more money to go to Australia than I was earning. In 2003, I thought, *Why stay in a hotel, when I could just rent a house?* Then I thought, *Hang on, why rent a house when I could buy a house?* So that's what I did. I bought my first place in Melbourne in 2003, initially just to save on the cost of hotels. Once I'd bought the place, I decided to make it feel more homely so that whenever I came to Australia, I was always coming home. Eric Powell already had a place on the Mornington Peninsular and so I bought my place in the same area. Having a place here meant that I could have the kind of lifestyle that I couldn't really have in the UK. I quickly bought a farm and built a studio there and with such amazing weather and very long, straight roads, it was the perfect place for my other passion: cars.

My sisters, Andrea and Pamela, were shocked when I told them I was buying a place in Australia. We'd all struggled together growing up, so to imagine that all this could come from my life in music was a lot to take in. Most of what we knew about Australia was from the movies, so when Pamela came on her first visit she was expecting a country filled with Crocodile Dundees and spiders and creepy-crawlies. It seemed a shame to disappoint her, so I prepared for her arrival by putting a fake snake in the garden and leaving it hidden in such a way that she would only see it when she was nearly on top of it. She arrived after an epic flight and headed over to the house. I was standing at the door as she walked up the path and she was nearly up to me with a big smile for her big brother, when out of the corner of her eyes she saw the snake. She screamed out: 'God!' - I remember thinking she should just call me Carl instead. It wasn't really the time for jokes because she was very, very angry, but I can say that out of the two of us 50 per cent found it hilarious. The snake has had many successes since then but now it's public knowledge I'll need to either find a different fake creature, or replace it with a real snake!

I'd had some great times out there. One New Year's Eve, I think it was 1996, I was playing with Darren Emerson from Underworld and we decided to head down to the Great Barrier Reef. We got to Port Douglas and who should we bump into but Pete Heller, who had been playing Cairns. So here we were, three British DJs, ready to go out and explore the Great Barrier Reef. So what did I do? I decided to somehow give myself a kidney stone, which meant that I spent the whole trip lying in bed in a hotel room. Every day, Darren and Pete would come back and tell me great stories about how they'd seen a manta ray and a starfish and a bloody seahorse and for all I knew a bloody mermaid too. I was pretty miserable. I've since been to the Great Barrier Reef many times, and it's an incredible place of wonder and beauty. If you get the chance to go there, you should take it. And please stop throwing your plastic bottles into the sea!

I started to get some of my DJ friends to join me at gigs. The scene was developing nicely in Australia and the clubbers were really receptive to new sounds. Laurent Garnier would always play with me when he was out there. I remember this one time when I asked him to tour Australia with me. The tour was great but as we got nearer to Sydney he told me there was a promoter who owed him money and that he wouldn't play for him. I just nodded my head, which to me meant 'I hear you' but to Laurent meant that I agreed. It just so happened that this promoter was part of the Sydney event, but I didn't think much of it until we were at the club. It was already jumping when we arrived and when we reached the DJ booth who should be standing in it but THAT promoter! Laurent went crazy with me and we had our first and only argument. He couldn't stay mad at me long, though, and a big hug at the end of the night sorted things out.

The country has just been ravaged by terrible fires, which show us how fragile the Earth is. I have my own little fire story from Australia. It was the mid-90s and we'd just done this big show in Adelaide. Normally I like to head off after my set, but there were a whole bunch of DJs that I wanted to catch up with so I went back to this apartment for the afterparty. We were all there chatting away when we suddenly heard sirens. Looking out over the balcony, I was confronted by thick smoke and my first thought was that the building was on fire. My second thought was: *Where are my records?*

What had actually happened was that someone at the party had flicked a cigarette from the balcony which landed on the back of a truck and had then caught fire. I don't know what was in that truck but the whole thing went up and the fire was still burning.

Sharing my music is something that I take very seriously, and over the years I've played to millions of people who have come to see me live and hopefully have taken a little bit of inspiration away with them.

Having guested on lots of radio stations, in 2001 I thought I'd try my hand at a little radio show of my own. What was meant to be something small and under the radar took on a life of its own. *Global* became the world's fastest-growing music show, getting up to 17 million listeners every week – the knock-on effect of this was to make me the most followed DJ on Mixcloud. The popularity of the show meant that I had to put more and more of my time into delivering something special. I'd always showcase music from my favourite labels and try to include a thirty-minute set from a guest DJ. I liked to end the show with a one-hour mix from me, either in the studio, or wherever I was on the road. Everyone knows that I can never say no to anything, but after sixteen years and 722 episodes I had to call it a day in 2017. Putting a show of this calibre together takes a lot of work, especially as it was going out on more than sixty stations across thirty-five territories, which involved making sure that music was accessible to an ever-growing and diverse audience. Having given so much of myself across the airwaves, my final two hours became a 'guilty pleasures' set. I played my favourite tunes from across three decades of music, and as I came to the end I started to get very emotional. For a moment I considered keeping the show running but, having achieved everything I set out to do with this, it was definitely the right decision to stop climbing this particular mountain. After all, when you plant your flag on top of Everest there is nowhere higher to go.

Eric Powell was working for a wine company and would go out looking at other wineries. I went with him on a couple of these road trips and on one particular day we drove through the gates of the Crittenden Estate. The place was beautiful, a lovely willow tree over the lake, it looked like the ideal place to experience life. On the way up, Eric and I had been talking about music, those old funk and soul and disco tracks. We both had all our records with us and reckoned it would be great to find a little place where we could have our own little party and play our own tracks to our friends. As if by magic, here we were, at the perfect spot. We somehow convinced the owners to let us throw a party there. They didn't want a rave and made us promise to keep the numbers small – about 150 people – which is exactly what we did. We thought we'd better give the party a name and, without having the benefit of an advertising agency, a PR company and numerous consultants, we came up with 'Carl and Eric's Mobile Disco'. For the first one, Eric and I set up on a veranda and tried to get people to go down to the patio below while we DJ'd up above. Now, people like to be where the action is, and so instead were crowding around the DJ set-up. The veranda was made of long planks of wood. Planks of wood are springy and bouncy, and as the people danced, it was jogging the vinyl and the needles were jumping all over the place. There aren't many times when you see DJs telling a packed dancefloor to stop dancing so vigorously. We tried again to get people down to the patio and eventually things settled down.

This night was so special, it was absolutely first rate. We had created the perfect combination of music, people and location, and we wanted to do this again. The landowner loved it and, because we'd been such good boys and had listened to everything he had said, he welcomed us back with open arms. Of course, next time we came back, we bought CDs with us instead of vinyl, which was a good job, as the veranda was even more bouncy, mainly because we had double the number of people.

The Mobile Disco is still going really well and Eric and I now get up to 6,000 people at each party. We play all across Australia and as far afield as Bali and New York. And we even have a band, MDFC, which stands for Mobile Disco Funk Connection, which we'd planned to tour, kicking off with a gig at London's Jazz Cafe in 2020, before heading across to play at Glastonbury. Not bad for a new band born out of a road trip to a winery in the back of beyond. Of course, the events of 2020 would make travel and performing live impossible.

The whole EDM thing seems to be everywhere. There were two big dance music events in Australia. One was called Stereosonic and the other was called Future Music, and these festivals had up to 60,000 people at them. They were pushing the EDM thing and had an audience who wanted it. I was always booked to headline the techno arenas, but they made these arenas very small, so they were always super-crowded and I felt were quite disappointing. Both these festivals ended up disappearing, which meant there was now no event where you could hear proper techno. So I decided to create my own techno festival-style event to plug the gap.

I wanted it to be all about the music, the DJs, the sound and the light. I wanted to take away the things that could cloud and overshadow these three things. So no CO_2 and no confetti cannons. I wanted to go back to the pure essence of what techno is all about. People often forget how important lighting is to setting the mood. A good DJ uses that alongside the music. If there is no lighting you might play your record in a slightly different way than if there's a full laser show around you. So: music, lights, live acts and DJs, and that's it.

I felt that other promoters were not remembering the reason why people go out. People go out to get lost in their emotions, to have shared experiences and to build memories. I wanted to take everyone back to where they needed to be, and that's why I launched the Pure festival in 2017. Pure is pure by name and pure by nature. I've been very careful to grow it organic-ally and to make sure that the music is at the forefront of the message. The great thing about lighting a bright candle like this is watching people coming. Like a moth to a flame, the right people have been attracted by this message. I do eight or nine Pure festivals per year in Australia, often in multiple cities across a two-week period.

With Pure and the Mobile Disco, I'm able to satisfy my own musical desires while I'm in Australia, which sets me up nicely for all the various shows I do across the world and keeps me working hard to deliver a personal dancefloor experience, no matter how big the crowd is. After all, I'm a clubber, just like you.

12.

The Playa

What keeps everything exciting to me is discovering new things: music, artists, technology and ways to share my sound. I've always thought that things need to start in the underground so they can filter up into the mainstream. As my career progressed, I learned that big is beautiful. My growing popularity meant that I was able to share my vision with a lot more people very quickly; working with excellent promoters who have given me free rein to do things my way, I've been able to do that.

The problem for me is that, as a DJ and producer, I'm always chasing that buzz. You know, the buzz when you hear a great piece of music for the first time, you're on the dancefloor dripping in sweat, surrounded by like-minded friends and having the time of your life. You never want it to end. The thing is, it does end. But that's OK, because next Saturday night, after a week of work, you can go out and do it all over again. The only thing is, if playing music *is* your work, you need that buzz every day. It's not just playing music but planning, discovering, connecting with people and all the things that form part of dance culture that I thrive on. Everywhere I go it's 'Coxy this' and 'Coxy that'. If I slip out to a club to check out some DJs I'm often bundled into some sort of roped-off VIP area and don't really get the full flavour of what the up-and-coming

DJs could do if left to their own devices. So when something spectacular happens, which it often does in this world, I try not to let it pass me by. I like to think of myself as a participant and not a bystander. I make sure to seize it with both hands.

I'd been hearing about this Burning Man thing from friends in the States. I didn't really get it. It seemed like some sort of hippy gathering that had been going on since the mid-80s and involved – as it said on the tin – a 'burning man' scarecrow moment. Burning Man had started as a ritual on the summer solstice when a bunch of friends set fire to a wooden effigy, a bit like a smaller version of *The Wicker Man*. This solstice party had a good vibe and in 1990 the organisers moved it into the desert a couple of hours north of Reno, Nevada, to a place called Black Rock, where it slowly grew year on year. It was a word-of-mouth thing, attracting creative types and freethinkers to the *playa* (dry lake bed). I was hearing about this in places like Ibiza and Germany at this point from people who were definitely cosmically out-there! Of course, at the same time, I was hearing about full-moon parties in Thailand, sunrise parties in Goa and desert raves in Israel.

I'm happy to play anywhere. I spend most of my time flying around the world and playing to incredible audiences so this was really just another possibility that was out there. But this Burning Man thing wouldn't go away. I guess my millennium gig with the whole Hawaii/Australia thing had captured people's imaginations. The world hadn't ended at midnight 1999 and suddenly, on what must have been a slow news day, everyone was talking about me. And I don't just mean the dance music press, I mean everyone. I started to get offered really interesting gigs and I think I could accurately say I was living the dream.

Living the dream is a weird phrase, because we're all living and we're all dreaming, but we're not all living the things we dream. I think about this a lot. Would I have been as happy in life if I'd stayed a shelf-stacker in a supermarket or a grass-cutter for the council or a scaffolder? I like to think I would have been happy, because I'm that kind of guy, but my dream was always to make and play music and share it with people. I am sure as hell doing that now. I was still hearing about this Burning Man thing. I'd see the odd picture in the papers and more and more people would tell me about this amazing experience and I was starting to think to myself that I really should have gone back in the day, but it's probably all over by now. Oh well, such is life.

By 2004 Burning Man had grown into a phenomenon. What started as a gathering of thirty-five people around an eight-foot wooden man (and wooden dog) had grown into a gathering of over 35,000 people and an 80-foot man. For once I felt like I had missed out.

Every time I'd thought of going in the past, I'd been busy or had come up with one excuse or another. Funnily enough, Paul Oakenfold had been going for years. By now he was living out in LA, producing pretty much everyone you've ever heard of, and would always unwind by heading out into the desert to reconnect and centre himself. Despite being music business through and through, Paul is a very spiritual guy and was really keen for me to join him so we could expand our hearts and minds together and share this experience. After the whole Venezuela thing in 2007, I felt I needed to get myself back on track and decided that I would finally hit Burning Man in 2008. It was a spontaneous choice - I decided on a Monday and on the Tuesday I was getting ready to go. Now most people that

I know can't just pick up and leave what they're doing. So after offers from loads of people to go to Burning Man with them, I ended up in 2008 going for my first time on my own. I finished my set in Ibiza, stuffed a few things in a backpack and went straight to the airport. People who know me know that when I'm spontaneous, I just plunge right in.

I'd heard that Burning Man had its own airport. But it turns out that by airport they mean airstrip and by airstrip they mean some land that had been levelled out in the middle of the desert. Obviously, there were no direct flights from Ibiza to Black Rock City. I flew from Ibiza to Gatwick and then straight on to Las Vegas. At Vegas, I switched to a flight to Reno, where I met some people who let me ride in their RV that was heading to the *playa*. This was some hard travelling. I'd been up all night in Ibiza and then spent hours at airports and on flights. I hadn't washed, I hadn't eaten (enough), and I was starting to wonder what the fuck I was doing here. I don't know what the opposite of spiritual is but I was definitely feeling that.

So, I was in the back of an RV, heading into the desert. It's pitch-black and as I looked out the window, I was definitely not feeling the vibe. The excitement of going in convoy to a rave back in the day was all about the shared adventure with the other revellers in their cars. Here we'd see a few vehicles heading our way but everything seemed very peaceful and quiet. Too quiet.

The first sign I had that something was cooking was at 2am when I saw some flickering lights in the distance. Now, if this was a proper rave, I'd expect to see laser lights, a Ferris wheel and probably hear the thumping bass. This looked like someone's gran was waving a candle and preparing to sing 'Auld

Lang Syne' in their living room. But as we all know, looks can be very deceptive. As we got closer, this little candle turned into a giant flame and when we turned onto a different angle, the flame became flames. The darkness, which I was getting used to, was dotted with fire, strange shadows and the sort of vehicle that thirty years earlier would have had the locals fearing an invasion from outer space. I felt like I'd landed on an alien surface. It wasn't of this world. It was mind-blowing! What the hell was going on? The most amazing-looking people, wearing the most outrageous outfits, were dancing, singing, skipping and celebrating. There was no pretension and everyone had checked their ego at the door. The only thing was, there was no door. So there I was, standing in a desert, in the dark, carrying a rucksack and wondering, *What do I do now?*

This was like nowhere else on earth. For sure, you could say this is a festival. In fact, I would call it *the* festival. One of the things that makes Burning Man really special are the camps. Some are tiny, others have their own stages, and some are focal points, and this is what I walked into. The dusty, windswept place with *Mad Max*-style vehicles, assorted cyber-punks and disco freaks, people from all over the world covered in face-paint and feathers giving off a primal energy that can only come from a shared collective experience like this. I was home.

I'd hooked up with a San Francisco crew who were running the Opulent Temple. They welcomed me into their camp and, of course, I played there. They were used to a more calm type of DJ, I think, because despite all the weirdness and madness going on around us, I blew their minds. I felt so energised that I gave them the full Coxy.

During my set I was tapped on the shoulder. Turning round, I saw a bloke wearing a blonde 'Heidi' wig, flip-flops and a

171

gold miniskirt. He was looking at me very strangely and I suddenly realised it was my old friend Matthew Benjamin, aka Bushwacka. I'd known Matthew since the rave days but had never seen him like this. I said, 'Alright, Matthew? How are you doing?' but he just stood and stared at me.

I found out from him later that he'd been at a wedding at another camp, United Nations, which had been pretty wild. Matthew had been sober for a year and hadn't realised that there were 'special' mushrooms in the food and liquid acid on the pasta, although I think the naked bridesmaids covered in glitter would have been an indication to proceed with caution. He'd ended up walking across the desert for two hours, guided by our lasers, until he saw thousands of people dancing. He arrived as our party was in full swing with me playing from a copper spaceship that was shooting out flames. Matthew found a ladder on the side and climbed into the spaceship, I imagine expecting to be transported to another planet, only to see me there.

The great thing was that everybody out here adds to the story. So being a DJ is not such a big deal and I could see that this was somewhere that I'd come to at the right moment for me. From the word go I was a full-on Burner. And I'm proud to say that I will be forever more.

I was welcomed back for the next few years at the Opulent Temple and I would always look to bring more and more of myself to my sets. It was a chance for them to experience my passion for music but it was also a chance for me to explore what I could do musically. This was not like any other outdoor festival experience I'd had before. The energy coming off the switched-on open-minded sea of party people pushed and pulled my creativity in different directions.

I'm a very good guest. You invite me to your house, I take my shoes off if asked, I always bring a bottle and I'm happy to help out in the kitchen. I like to think that alongside my sparkling wit and dashing looks, I leave every place happier than when I found it. While I was loving being a guest at Burning Man and playing for my new Burner family, I felt I could give a lot more. And somehow, the idea of creating my own camp started to take shape.

Anyone that knows me or knows of me knows what I love: music, partying, dancing, people and having fun. My first Burning Man experience was all of these things. No one could have told me how amazing it was going to be and if they had done I don't think I would have believed them. I do wish I'd done a bit more planning and checked out the environment as most of my favourite T-shirts were destroyed with the thick desert dust. But suddenly, I felt I'd discovered something that I didn't even know I was missing. So this is it, this is where we are now, a place where people can come together, throw away their inhibitions and be themselves. At Burning Man, you can only keep up an act for so long; with a mouth full of dust, and so much to see and do, you can only be yourself.

And I realised I could *really* be myself, experiment musically and have fun with people from every corner of the world who I would never normally get to meet, all of us being blown away by the creativity that we were surrounded by. I knew I would want to come back here every year so it made sense to see if I could set up my own camp at Burning Man.

With most festivals, my manager can pick up the phone and everything I need, from production and technical to hospitality, is sorted. Burning Man is a whole new world. Actually, make that a whole new universe. It's not about what Burning Man can do for us but what we can do for Burning Man. So what could I do? I could bring good music, good vibes, a big smile and energy that hopefully could add to the experience. It was time to put in some calls.

Amazingly, no one tried to talk me out of it, no one groaned and no one told me I was crazy. Everyone jumped at the chance to make this happen. There were already lots of dance acts popping up at Black Rock City and you could see guys like Armin van Buuren, Oakey, Freq Nasty and François Kevorkian at various camps. I wanted my own camp but I wanted it to be massive, with phenomenal sound, great visuals and the best line-ups. Part of the Burning Man ethos is about 'leaving no trace', so this would be a proper in-and-out job, and coming from the rave scene I knew all about this. I'd have to put it all together, get everyone down there, set it all up, then take it all down and get rid of it all to the point where it looked like we were never there. And, of course, pay for it all! This is where having a PhD in rave-ology comes into its own. I know how to get into a field, build a sound system, fill it with party people, take it all down, clean it all up and disappear without a trace.

Of course, to get to that point for an illegal rave, I'd have had to drive around the countryside being followed by undercover police and send covert messages to 20,000 ravers to try to get them to turn up at the right place, at the right time, on the right day. So doing this in the desert should be a walk in the park.

I was so excited that even before we'd worked out all the logistics, I was already asking friends to come and play alongside me. I figured that I couldn't or wouldn't or shouldn't play five days straight and needed to make sure that my camp stood out for quality and creativity. The Playground was born. We started looking at what we would need to make this work. Pioneer would supply a sound system and make sure the sound quality was optimal throughout the whole festival. This has turned out to be one of the strangest loans in sound-system history. They lend us the system on the basis that they will take it back at the end of the event. But the amount of dust blowing across the player means that by the last day, the system is not repairable – every part of it is filled with dust, so it's thrown away. This means that every year, I go back to Pioneer, who are delighted to loan me the sound system to be used at Burning Man on the basis that they will get it back in one piece as promised, whereupon they take one look at it and write it off. I'm sure they're delighted to learn that I intend to run the Playground forever and ever and ever.

I spend a lot of time thinking about what I'm going to play and who I want to book for the Playground. I normally have at least one of my sets streamed, so I need to make sure to capture the spirit of Burning Man but make it accessible to a wide, global audience who want to feel the energy taking place all around us in the desert through their screens.

There are a lot of distractions at Burning Man. Did I mention the dust? It is bloody everywhere. It has a way of getting through your clothes, through your skin and right into your soul. It's the only way to explain it. The thing is, with nature, there's no point fighting it. You just have to embrace it; in a way, the dust makes Burning Man what it is. No roped-off VIP room here with a sharp-suited club pimp clutching his bottle of champagne, surrounded by dolly birds. Here we all wear the same thing, white dust. And, boy, do we wear it well.

To be fair, I do put some effort into what I wear at Burning Man. People are way-out here, so much so that if aliens decided to land, someone would go up to them and say, 'Nice outfit, make a bit more effort next time.' I try to keep it subtle, something basic, like a fluffy pink sheepskin jacket, my *Mad Max* dust-repellent goggles, a casual pair of silver-mirrored cowboy boots and something low-key like a mad hatter's top hat plonked on my head – after all, I wouldn't want to look ridiculous! I always end up with a feather boa or two around my neck and make sure my outfit is topped off by a nice, subtle two-inch-thick coating of – yes, you guessed it – dust. People go all out to express themselves and, as a people-watcher, I really see the crowd coming into their own; for many of them, this is the escape that they want and need.

Every year at Burning Man is like a new adventure. You start off checking out the whole site and the amazing sculptures that reflect the essence of the founders of Burning Man. It's so well organised. Black Rock City is exactly that, a city. It might be a new city that springs up every year following a theme and is then dismantled, but a city it is. It has streets on a grid system, it has its own airport (sort of), many camps and villages, and an impressive focal point, which is the Man itself. It's as if a higher power has cherry-picked all the fun and interesting people and transported them into the desert. Everyone gets something different out of their experience and deep, long-lasting friendships are built there. When it's time to go, they really do mean 'leave no trace'. Much of the production is built in an ethical way and is burnt onsite, with even the burn-scars then being removed. The environment is a fragile thing and even water cannot be dumped on the *playa*. Used shower water needs to either be evaporated off or taken home with you, and when you see how spotless Black Rock City is and then think of the rubbish left at places like

Glastonbury and Tomorrowland, you wonder why people can't do this everywhere.

I have had some of my maddest experiences at Burning Man. But you know what they say, what happens at Burning Man stays at Burning Man. But it's not Vegas. Burning Man is like one big shared secret, with all of us Burners being part of this amazing story. I've been running my camp since 2015 and it just gets bigger and bigger. Whenever I need a boost I sit down and think about what I can add to the next Burning Man. I'm so proud that I have created what I believe to be the perfect Playground for adults and I feel so grateful to have been welcomed into Burning Man with open arms. I know that anyone who comes is there for the right reasons and is probably the kind of person who I'd want to sit down with, lift up my goggles, rub a damp flannel over my face, look them in the eye and say, 'Hey, nice to meet you.'

So if you're reading this and you come to Burning Man, come over and see me. Stretch your legs on my dancefloor, kick up some dust, hang out and join us. See you on the *playa*.

13.

We Conquered

The new millennium was filled with opportunity for everyone in the electronic music world. We had ridden the waves and landed on the sandy beach – we had made it. The culture had exploded and in a good way.

It was like everything had been building to the year 2000 and what would follow. Youth culture had come to dominate in a positive way, with the promoters and DJs who had got going in the early days putting on more and more impressive and ambitious events. We'd gone global, with outposts all over the world and electronic music fortresses wherever you looked. New York, Ibiza, Liverpool, Berlin, Rimini – we were like Genghis Khan's hordes, unstoppable. While we were pushing boundaries outwards, the powers that be had decided to celebrate the millennium in the world's cultural epicentre, London, by building the Millennium Dome and filling it with exhibits that wouldn't have been out of place in the 1950s. This was the same story across the planet – they didn't reach out to the dance generation and we didn't feel included in the festivities. Perhaps we were already too far away to reach. In any case, we didn't care. We had our thing going on.

It wasn't long before the cultural importance of dance music had reshaped the entertainment industry. The influence of those small clubs, a handful of DJs and a bunch of ravers experimenting with fashion and brands meant that dance music had the potential to go big. The rave scene brand had the best advertising of all. National newspapers running front-page stories showing young people having the time of their lives made everyone want to try this out. And once they'd tried it out, there was no going back. They certainly weren't going to flock to anything like the Millennium Dome.

The press got it wrong about us most of the time. It caused us all a lot of problems, but in the end they poured fuel on the fire they were trying to extinguish. They thought they'd finish us off but they just made us bigger and better. In 1990 my name was splashed on flyers for underground raves. Nearly a decade on I was on posters on the London Underground.

I was about to star in a movie about that very culture that would be screened at proper cinemas. Not some art-house screening at the back of a club, but the kind of place where your folks might go with a box of popcorn. The film, of course, was *Human Traffic*. The director was gunning for me and wanted me to be in the film, not as a DJ but as an actor - I was gonna play a club owner. Just before I signed the contract, though, the studio behind the film got a little bit nervous. After all, I'm a DJ not an actor. They made me come in for a screen test, which must have gone OK as it wasn't long before I was on the screen as Pablo Hassan, club owner. It was great being at the premiere in June 1999 as part of the crew — there's a real buzz on the red carpet. Everyone tries to get a sound bite out of you and I remember this journalist wanted me to say, 'Just say no to drugs,' and me thinking that if you're talking to your drugs you're already too far gone. It was a lot of fun but that's all it was. Fame for fame's sake isn't for me. When it comes to entertaining people I'm about three things: music, music and music!

I felt like I had it all going on just as I would have wanted it – even more so. I was playing all over the world alongside the most talented artists and on the best sound systems. You'd turn up at an airport and see someone with some record boxes and straight away you'd start a conversation before heading off in different directions clutching a pile of magazines like *Jockey Slut*, *7*, *Mixmag* and *DJ Mag* as you headed out to your gig. Those flights to Ibiza were a nightmare as we all fought for the overhead space to put our boxes and bags, jostling for space with record-company types with boxes of promos and bags of duty-free. Other than the Ibiza flights you were normally the only DJ on the plane and I had a few inflight conversations explaining to whoever was sitting next to me that yes, I was a DJ, but no, I wasn't on the radio.

Our numbers continued to expand. The festival scene was growing, and the scale of the line-ups meant we were often travelling together. Even festivals like Exit in Serbia had grown so quickly – from a standing start in 2000 as a protest by a bunch of students against the government to a major festival – that there could be twenty artists on your flight alone. I guess it was a natural progression. Now these events were licensed and legal, and with so many great artists out there, the demand was there. Once the whole internet and online thing kicked in, promoting internationally in real time became easier and the festival scene dominated the musical landscape. When I first played Glastonbury in 1994 it was revolutionary. To a lot of people dance music wasn't real music – where were the guitars, and how come the drumming was coming out of a computer? If anyone could make this music in their bedroom then maybe anyone could make this music. Dance music was given its own space, a dance stage or possibly a little arena in some far-flung corner of the festival.

Even in 2008, when Jay-Z headlined Glastonbury there was huge criticism of the choice. He may have been one of the biggest artists on the planet and by then had won six Grammy Awards and been nominated for nineteen more, but he was a hip-hop artist so it 'isn't real music'. He opened his set with his version of 'Wonderwall' by Oasis and, despite having a tough time, I feel he won over the crowd, and the critics. Glastonbury sells out every year before they announce the line-up and a lot of thought goes into it, so you have to applaud this choice. It opened up possibilities for every genre to enjoy an audience of music lovers. By 2019, when Stormzy headlined in his Banksy Union Jack stab vest, no one batted an eyelid. As my mate Norman says, 'We've come a long way, baby.'

When we started out the DJ was normally in the darkest corner of the club. It was as if the club owners forgot about the music and shoved us in as an afterthought. Now we are centre stage! When dance music really broke through in America there were some promoters who saw what we'd done and incorporated that into what they were doing. We fought for the scene in the UK in the same way that they would fight to build something in the USA that they believed in. A good example of this are the promoters Disco Donnie and Pasquale Rotella, who after many ups and downs came together to create the Electric Daisy Carnival. EDC has gone on to become one of the most important festivals for the electronic music community. Dance music in America was given a massive boost when it finally broke into the charts in a major way. French DJ David Guetta's collaboration with the Black Eyed Peas, 'I Gotta Feeling', brought dance music to the masses. People who were listening to pop music were suddenly, almost without realising it, listening to electronic music, not aware of the significance of what had happened in Chicago and Detroit, as UK DJs started to get lots of bookings in the States. We were basically bringing house and techno back to the country it originated from, a bit like when the Rolling Stones originally toured in the USA – they reintroduced their support acts like B.B. King to the country that originated the blues.

A lot of festivals are quite compact – you can get around them very easily. Ultra in Miami is the opposite, as far as festivals go – it's a monster. This is where I have my own stage, known as the Carl Cox Megastructure. It's a 45-minute walk from my stage to the main stage so I need to work hard to keep my crowd rocking. It started as a one-day thing, moved to two days and now it's three, and it's bigger and louder than ever before. The scale of it allows them to bring in guests across every genre of dance music and I can share the bill with old and new friends across multiple genres like Pete Tong, Afrojack, Steve Aoki and David Guetta.

I've been really lucky that the organisers give me free rein (and a healthy budget) to programme with, and I use the opportunity to push boundaries, especially now I have the opportunity to introduce the new generation of EDM-following Americans to the music I play and the way I play it. They may not recognise most of the tunes I'm dropping, but the energy catches them and draws them in.

The standout guest for me was Laurent Garnier in 2011. I've known Laurent for a long time and we've played at a lot of clubs together, including Ultimate and Le Rex. By the time

I asked him to play Ultra they were trying to scale the sets down so that people didn't play for more than a couple of hours. This meant they could have more artists on the line-up. I imagine they thought that more artists on the bill would mean faster ticket sales.

For me a two-hour set feels too short. I try to put myself on the dancefloor and imagine what it must feel like to be really getting into your groove and then for the music to switch, which changes the energy and your mood. I'm not saying that everyone should do a mega-set, but I think the promoters should get the right balance between quantity and quality when it comes to their line-ups. My longest sets have been ten hours! After ten hours even I'm done - my legs and back are killing me and my brain is pretty much fried. I think that length of set is my limit. Being a DJ, no matter how much fun it is, is still a job. Most people go to work for eight hours and during that time they have a couple of tea breaks, a lunch break, maybe go for a smoke or two, enjoy a bit of office banter and before they know it they're out of the door. Now imagine doing a full working day standing up and concentrating without anything to eat and not even having the chance to go to the loo! Welcome to my world.

Now Laurent has a similar outlook - he is not just a craftsman, he's a master craftsman, and insisted that if he couldn't play four to five hours he wouldn't play at all. This made sense to me; I rarely put my foot down but, when I do, I like to think that the shock waves shake things up and make things happen. In this case, I didn't have to stomp, the guys behind Ultra are also all about the music and got it straight away. The want the best and they had Laurent Garnier offering them his services. A no-brainer, obviously.

Right from the start Laurent was drawing people in with his sound. The only way we were able to get this mega-set into the line-up was for Laurent to start the festival, so he played at the beginning to an empty arena as the gates opened. From the word go you could see the crowd responding to his playing in a different way to how you'd expect them to behave with an opening act. Normally you get to a festival and you wander around looking at all the things on offer and working out what you're gonna be doing; but I could see that the audience had come to dance. Three hours in and Laurent was totally lost in his music and was clearly on a journey, with the whole crowd as his passengers.

You hear DJs talking about taking people on a journey a lot; the phrase is a cliché because, in reality, the crowd find their own way and while the DJ might think they are going places together, it doesn't mean the crowd is there with him. But in this case, the lucky party goers were on the mother of all journeys. Four hours in and with the place absolutely packed, Laurent had them eating out of the palm of his hand. By the time he got through to his fifth hour, he had blown everyone away, including all the other artists that had come to watch this genius at work. I always close the stage and I can honestly say that a lot of my inspiration that day came from what I had just witnessed. Laurent left a legacy behind with that set and gave the Americans a crash course in techno that they could understand. Loco Dice came on next, followed by me and we were riding high on the energy that Laurent had created.

These festivals are like being part of a mini-town that springs up with its infrastructure and regulations and then disappears again after the event. Looking after the festival goers is one thing, but looking after the artist is a whole other operation.

We are all coming and going, often performing there as part of a bigger tour and being ferried backwards and forwards on very tight schedules. Now that we're not all lugging record boxes around there's a lot less that can go wrong, but the potential for disaster is always just around the corner.

I've had a few lucky escapes myself. The most serious was in 2018. I was set to fly from Buenos Aires to Uruguay on a private jet - the plane was on the runway and heading into position to take off. As it picked up speed, the outside cabin door suddenly flung open and the pilot seemed unaware of this. Luckily the cockpit door was open so I started waving and shouting at the pilot, who just waved and smiled back. I was really screaming at him so I could be heard over the engine noise and luckily got his attention, so he could stop the plane. Everyone on the plane was shaken but the pilot just laughed it off, the doors closed and we took off - it must have happened to him all the time.

Everything *should* run smoothly but - life being what it is and humans being who they are - sometimes things just happen. I was in Brazil in 2016 for Ultra and the day before the festival I went out socialising with the promoters and their friends. This wasn't just the Ultra guys but also the local promoters, who wanted to make sure that we had a great time. You hear stories about some of these places being quite dangerous but when you're with people who know the score you rarely have a thing to worry about. Unless you go out of your way to piss someone off and pick a fight. And that's exactly what happened to us. Within our group was the girlfriend of one of the local promoters. She stood out because she was really brash and even though I couldn't really understand what she was saying, I could see how rude she was to the bar staff and to people who weren't in our group. She started arguing with

B2B with Norman Cook aka Fatboy Slim in 2019. © Alon Shulman / Photo: Dan Reid

We did it! Live with Paul Oakenfold and Alon Shulman at Stonehenge.
© Alon Shulman

'That's all, folks!' The last tune plays out on the last night at Space. © Dan Reid

The last night at Space. © Dan Reid

With Pepe as the music stops on the last night at Space. © Dan Reid

At Kappa with Amelie Lens. © Dan Reid

Kappa Festival, Turin, provides one of the most satisfying DJ booth views.
© Ian Hussey

Crashing into world champion Valentino Rossi on the dancefloor.
© Carl Cox

Now that's what I'm talking about!
© Aaron Staples Photography

235mph in my main drag car, Eleanor.
© Harley Stephens

Me and Eleanor.
© Carl Cox

Carl Cox Motorsports in action in New Zealand.
© Mad Love Media

Trackside in Australia. © Mad Love Media

The Cox family in Australia. © Carl Cox

Having a meeting on the Playa - with Ian Hindmarsh at Burning Man. © Ian Hindmarsh

One Night Stand at Amnesia. © Manel Gimeno

Cabin Fever – the Vinyl Sessions. © World Famous Promotions / Zenith Watches

Time Warp in Mannheim: 4am on 7 April 2019 - an 'Oh yes, oh yes!' moment. © Ian Hindmarsh

Hard at work in the studio. © World Famous Promotions / Zenith Watches

the security guard at the bar, and I don't know how things escalated so quickly, but the next thing a few more security guards came over and tried to get to the girl. I didn't have a clue what was going on but as things heated up between our group and these guards I found myself with everyone else running down the street being chased. It was very strange because I was running away from something I didn't understand just because some people I didn't really know but was hanging out with were running away from them. I wasn't sure what would happen if I stopped running but I didn't want to find out. We ended up barricading ourselves in a garage under a building with the security guards trying to get in from the outside. I don't know what she said to them but that girl must have really pissed them off. Luckily for us, people from the building came down and let us out through a different door.

Sometimes problems arise that seem unsolvable, which is why I feel lucky to have some very lateral-thinking people around me. I very rarely cancel a show and when I have it's almost always been through things out of my control. When I did my B2B set with Fatboy Slim in London in 2019 I had a high temperature but was always going to be there. I've always been able to find inner strength when it comes to music. For me, cancelled shows are normally down to airlines. In the summer of 2019 I was in Ibiza and due to fly to Italy via Madrid. The Ibiza flight was delayed, which meant I couldn't make the Madrid connection and there were no other flights that day. This wasn't a small club gig I was heading to - it was a stand-alone Carl Cox show on the beach at Jesolo near Venice in front of a sell-out crowd of 15,000 people. My tour manager, Ian Hussey, had to deal with a very frantic promoter and I was pleased that Ian was able to calm him down so they could

187

work on a solution. We tried everything, but no airline was available from anywhere. In the end the promoter managed to find a private jet, which was a massive twenty-seater, that flew the two of us to the gig in time for the show. I still can't believe that the promoter pulled this off, but I'm sure that 15,000 potential refunds was a great motivator.

Following the tragedy on the dancefloor in Venezuela and my initial shock I had felt able to continue the tour. I owe a lot of that resolve to being with my parents in Barbados. The drama that can be stirred up by the industry melted away and I came to see that it was simply a case of being in the wrong place at the wrong time. I'd taken it very personally but on reflection I felt sorry for the victims and the circumstances that made something so terrible possible. Seeing my parents in their beloved Barbados put everything in perspective and helped me focus on what I wanted to achieve. I went back to South America and I knew I was going to be well looked after. I was able to focus on my trademark big smile and the energy that I can bring to the dancefloor. One of the shows was in Medellín in Colombia. There was so much rain coming down that the car got stuck and I couldn't get anywhere near the stage for the festival I was booked at. So I ended up rocking up on the back of a filthy tractor driven by a farmer. The show was great, though, and the audience were really receptive to my music. What had happened in Venezuela had obviously made all the press, so the audience had gone out of their way to make me feel extra welcome.

When we got to the capital, Bogotá, I was taken to one of the top restaurants, which was excellent. It was full of families enjoying their dinner and there was some salsa music playing in the background. The owner came up to me and I stood up to shake his hand; as I did so he handed me a pair of maracas, signalled for the music to go louder and put me to the front of the restaurant, which I now realised was a stage. So there I was, shaking the maracas while everyone at the restaurant got up and started dancing. And I don't just mean polite bopping, people were dancing on the tables and going wild. Once again, Carl just can't say no.

Despite what had happened in Venezuela, the next gig was probably the most dangerous show of my life and I can't imagine ever being in a hotter situation. The show was at a venue outside of Bogotá that had been built by a local businessman to be a replica of the Taj Mahal. The party was inside and there was a huge spiral ramp going all the way up to the VIP area at the top. The crowd was great and the party was awesome, and after my set I was led up to the VIP area. There was a real atmosphere up there, and not a very happy one. It turned out, so the promoters told me, that this was the first time the leaders of the three biggest Colombian drug cartels had been seen in public together. All these guys were fans and had come out to hear me play. This was a *very* heavy room, full to capacity, mobbed in every sense of the word. I was treated really well, but was still very pleased to be out of there.

Festivals today are so professionally done that almost nothing can go wrong. It's not like the good old days when there was so much to worry about before you got to the event. Now all events, from the small to the mega, have a certain formula they like to stick to. There is a perceived way of doing things that works and that the crowds expect to be in place. That being said, it doesn't hurt to shake things up a little bit and alter people's expectations.

Tomorrowland is one of those festivals that always gets it right. Held in the appropriately named town of Boom in Belgium, they are the kind of organisation that could write a rulebook on how to put on the perfect festival. Their success is based on doing things differently and, as the name implies, they are always looking to the future. It's the perfect place to shake things up a little bit.

I told them I was interested in opening the festival, which was unusual because the headliner never opened, traditionally there'd be a build-up with the headliner coming on towards the end of the show. Most headliners like to go on very late when the crowd is ready for them but I felt that by going on at the very beginning and playing on the main stage I could help set the mood for the day. I played my first tune at midday from the main stage at exactly the moment the festival gates opened. This means that at the very start of the set I was playing to zero people. Once the gates were open, the crowd instinctively headed straight to the main stage and it was like seeing a tidal wave heading over the hills towards me. By the end of my three-hour set I had an audience of over 50,000 people in front of me – I had built the mood from a standing start. It worked so well that I've been doing this at Tomorrowland for the last few years.

Having control over a line-up means that I can really mix it up to make sure the people dancing in front of us have the best time possible. I like to book DJs with integrity, who are not afraid of taking risks and try to push themselves at every stage. Even the big promoters are happy for me to do things my way, as they can see that I am genuinely doing what I feel will enhance the audience experience.

When Cream took over Finsbury Park in 2019 for Creamfields London and built their massive Steel Yard structure, they put

Eric Prydz on the Saturday with his full-on laser light show. I took over Sunday with a tribute to Space in Ibiza. Within my line-up I brought in Clara Da Costa, Nic Fanciulli, Steve Lawler and Eats Everything. To mix it up, I put Eats on in the middle of the day and curated my line-up so that together we could all build a story and the party flowed smoothly from beginning to end. It was an early finish, with me closing the stage when my set ended at 10pm. The applause from the 15,000-strong crowd who were about to descend on the local tube station was not just for me. The cheering was for the whole line-up and, in the spirit of what I do and the way I do it, all of us DJs stood together to share in the praise.

One of the roles of a headliner is to make that dancefloor explode, because you're not only showcasing yourself, but the promoter and the party. This has made a lot of DJs lazy, because the easiest way to keep the momentum going is just to play those big familiar tunes. There is a certain thing to be said for playing very popular tracks but - a bit like a sugar rush - the buzz fades very quickly. I have always used my position to challenge people's expectations and believe that my sound does as much for the dancefloor as just sticking on a big tune and pressing 'play'.

Having so much access to digital music means that I've been able to scale down my compulsive record buying, which is lucky because it had gone out of control. I don't know exactly how many I have but it's at least 150,000 pieces of vinyl and they're all within easy reach. I love music across every genre but my favourite album is still *Songs in the Key of Life* by Stevie Wonder. I was always buying records to play and not just to collect. Some of those serious DJ record collectors like Norman

Jay and Gilles Peterson would be horrified at the state of some of my rare funk tracks that used to get quite a lot of battering during my early sets.

My record collection starts from about 1963 with my dad's records and goes through solidly until 2006, when I stopped buying records (although I still get sent vinyl, most of which I add to the collection). I shudder to think what I must have spent, but I have played every single one at some point. When I decided to ship them out to Australia I needed two 20-foot containers.

The transition from playing on CDs to digital was pretty smooth – much easier than when the CDs started to replace turntables. A lot of people were quite snobbish about vinyl and felt that a DJ using CDs was somehow less real. I'd agree there is something more satisfying about holding and owning a piece of vinyl. It is a thing of beauty. But when it comes to DJing it's all about how people react to the music. The format doesn't matter, because the music is what it's all about. It might feel more satisfying to read a story from a rare first edition, but the listener should be getting the same enjoyment from the words no matter what version they've got.

Having started on the lowest rung of the ladder and climbed up bit by bit, I feel that I grew into the festival mindset, which is very different to playing in a club environment. By contrast, today's artist almost needs to be main-stage-ready from day one.

When the USB stick first came in they took some getting used to. We'd just about managed to ride the vinyl to CD wave – they were both round and you were manipulating the music that was in front of you. Now it was a little stick full of music. You could carry several record boxes around in your pocket and so could everyone else. USBs all looked fairly similar and it was very common, especially with three or four players in front of you, for someone to pull out the wrong stick. This happened to me a lot. I would be just getting underway when the person on before me would pull out what they thought was their stick to find the whole venue go silent. The crossover became a nightmare, and there were even stories of audience members grabbing sticks and legging it. Nowadays, USB sticks are colour-coded, so all of us on the line-up only have to remember which colour we are and hope that the other DJs remember which colour they are.

The way that the dance music industry embraced new technology was always going to be something that propelled the scene forward quickly and allowed us to overtake other cultural fields in terms of growing our audience. We didn't have to adapt or worry about change – we got going from a standing start and had nothing to lose. Our little movement became a scene before becoming an industry and with the wealth of emerging talent and the ever-growing audience it is safe to say that its influence has conquered the world.

It takes a lot of experience to be able to read a crowd and understand what needs to happen to make that dancefloor respond in the way you want it to. It's a learning process and you're always trying to improve. Some of the newer DJs hoping to break through haven't learned the craft and they've let the technology that is available now do it for them. You can't blame them, after all, this is the technology that existed when they came in. Of course, you'd use any technology that's available to you but, a bit like a Jedi Master, it's important to follow your instincts and make sure that you are controlling the technology and the technology is not controlling you. The key is to focus on the music and always remember that the crowd is the star. Use the Force!

14.

Let's Go!

I've always been obsessed with cars and bikes. When you've got no money and you're buying cars that cost less than a good pair of trainers, you have to learn how to take things apart and put them back together (a bit like sound systems). I'm interested in how things work and what I can do to enhance them.

My first real car was a Mini, which was actually made up of two Minis. I had bought them both for the combined price of £60. One of them had a good body but a non-existent engine and the other one had a really good engine but was covered in dents (and the dents were covered in rust and the rust was covered in scratches and it looked like somebody had whacked in a few more dents to finish the look). My first project was making these two cars into one car. I didn't have a garage or access to anywhere to do the work, so it was all done in my front yard, which meant that I had to carry all the parts and tools that weren't attached to the car itself into the house every night. Eventually, it was ready! I painted it bright orange and it had lovely wheels. It wasn't perfect - for example, when I put my foot down, the radiator would rub against the side of the car - but it was mine. I had this car for a year and a half and eventually sold it for £100.

As a kid, I'd gone to Brands Hatch a few times to check out the various motorsport events. I would normally go on the days when they were desperate for a crowd and it was cheap or even free to get in, so I got to see a lot of very strange car races and motorbikes with sidecars whizzing round the track.

Despite my size, I love riding motorbikes. I've always had a lot of respect for bikers and if I wasn't a DJ, I think I would have tried to make it as a rider myself. I would DJ regularly in Gisborne, New Zealand, and I had this idea to ride from Auckland to Gisborne on a motorbike for my next gig. I'd met a DJ there called Gavin when I was playing at Rhythm and Vines in Gisborne and he was really into bikes. He was involved with a sidecar team and our shared love of bikes turned into a conversation that resulted in me getting into the whole racing thing.

I was keen to get involved without falling into a money pit, so my first step was some historic bike racing, where I rode my GSX-R 1989 Suzuki. I really got into it very quickly. I'd missed all this while I was DJing in the early years because I'd kept my head down and just focused on my music. Now that a lot of the logistics of my global career are being taken care of by other people, I have the time to devote to music and motorsport. As of 2020, I have a whole bunch of bikes that I race and each one has its own nickname, personality, and gives me a little something different. It's a bit like B.B. King and Eric Clapton naming their favourite guitars.

I liked the idea of getting involved with a sidecar team because it was very grassroots and the kind of racing that doesn't get much media attention. People don't know much about it, but it's very skilful and getting into it really excited me. Sponsoring a couple of riders gave me a very nice little entry into that world and I met some great people. They were amazed that I had so much mechanical knowledge and that I could also ride.

As things progressed, and I needed to separate Carl Cox the DJ from Carl the petrol head, I developed a separate identity, Carl Cox Motorsport, which we established in 2013. I also set up the CCM Cup in New Zealand, which sponsors young riders at entry level; I could see that helping to nurture up-and-coming talent could lead to great things for them. As an international DJ, I was getting invited to F1 and Superbikes events and I was meeting other dance music artists who were also interested in the sport, like Keith Flint.

There is actually an Ibiza connection to how I got back into biking. I was having dinner at Las Dos Lunas with my booking agent Ian Hindmarsh and going through the European dates for that year. It wasn't a typical meeting because there were about twenty of us at the table and someone started talking about motorbikes. Ian casually mentioned that he had a Harley-Davidson V-Rod, which is a very sexy-looking bike. I just said, 'Get the fuck out of here!' He didn't have any photos with him and told me it was in Barcelona and I was welcome to check it out. It sounded like a tall story to me. Imagine his surprise when two days later I turned up in Barcelona ready to see this beauty. I hadn't been on a bike since I was a teenager . . . but for some reason I decided that maybe Ian didn't need to know that. As I got on the Harley and started riding down the coast road I sensed he was a little bit suspicious, especially as I was still wearing flip-flops. Just to make sure I could really ride, he was following me in his Jeep. When I got to the end of the road I couldn't turn the bike around because it was so narrow there. I had to do a biker's version of a three-point turn so we could head back to the place we'd agreed I would pull over. Ian knows me very well, so he probably wasn't surprised when I didn't stop and instead rode off into the distance. I loved it, and started taking the various tests I needed to be able to ride any bikes I wanted so I could get a bike or two of my own. This hobby has turned into a passion and, including what I have with the team, I now have over sixty bikes.

Carl Cox Motorsport was still really a hobby and could quite easily have stayed that way, because I was really enjoying what I was doing. In 2014, I had the opportunity to enter my sidecar team at the Isle of Man TT, which gave me a taste of what it would be like to be at the next level while putting me in front of the racing community. I was like a kid in a sweet shop and have never looked back. I've just got more and more involved as time has progressed.

We were very lucky to get Michael Dunlop in as a rider for the 600cc Supersport class. Michael comes from the famous Dunlop motorsport family and his father, uncle and brother have all tragically been killed racing. Despite this, he never holds back. I'd been playing in Ibiza and flew to the Isle of Man and headed over to the paddocks. As I got there, Michael, who I'd never met before, was just going up onto the grid. He came over and shook my hand. There are times when you wish you had planned what you are going to say. And if I had planned it, I might have said something motivational or something that would show I knew my stuff. Instead, I actually said, 'Give them shit,' to which he replied, 'I will, boss.' He promptly went on to win the race. So there I was, standing in the winner's circle, with a big smile on my face.

I have great fun on the Isle of Man and get great support there. One of the riders, called Connor, has supported me from day one and he asked me if I could play a bit of music for him. This turned out to be one of the oddest parties I've ever played at. It was basically a pop-up party in a coffee shop for fifty people, which was the capacity. There was no booze, so if you wanted a drink you had to go to the Co-op across the road, pick up a bottle and bring it back. There were no doormen and all the riders came down. Condensation was dripping from just about everywhere onto just about every-thing and everyone. I played a four-hour set and could have gone on forever. Now, although I was doing this for shits and giggles, the policy that I adopted from those early rave days when I would get stiffed is that I always make sure I get paid. Connor paid me in coffee and I think I ended up with at least half a jar, which seemed like a fair swap!

This kind of camaraderie among the riders reminds me a lot of the early days of dance music and was one of the reasons why I bought my house on the Isle of Man. I try and go to the Manx Classic every September as well as the TT in June, and even though I'm always adamant that I will not play, the fact that I have a sound system there packed up and ready to go, and with my music always on me or near me, tells me that even I don't believe that I'm just there for the bikes.

Riding gives me a sense of freedom that I don't really get anywhere else. There are no texts or emails and with my helmet on I'm not on show. Maybe that's why Daft Punk do it! I spend most of my working life surrounded by people, so getting on my bike gives me that solitude that lets me focus on myself and gives me time for my own thoughts. Spending much of 2020 in lockdown made me realise how much I missed riding on the open road and I started to bring some of the bikes into the house. Having my MV Agusta, which is like a work of art, in the kitchen helps me start the day on a positive.

I had a lucky escape once on a quad bike out in Uruguay. I was on tour and had stopped off to see Ian Hindmarsh, who'd emigrated from Newcastle and lives in quite a remote spot out there with his family. It turned out that the pop star Shakira lives somewhere up the mountain in a massive mansion, and Hindmarsh, Hussey and I decided that it might be fun to ride up and take a look. We headed up the dirt roads with both the Ians on the back of one bike, as the other one had broken down. We didn't really know where we were going and there definitely wasn't anyone you could ask, so we managed to take the wrong path and end up at the wrong house.

The house had a driveway with a roundabout in the middle, so they drove through to turn around and I followed. Security is a big thing out there, but Ian Hindmarsh didn't look worried and, I figured, as he knew the score, why should I be? What I didn't know was that this house was guarded by a massive Rottweiler who had been woken up by the first bike, so as I came around it was on full alert. It started chasing me and just wouldn't give up. I was on full throttle with this dog nipping my heels and barely managed to get away. At some of those original raves, the ones where the security was trying to get heavy, I always steered clear of the guys who had Rottweilers - and here I was in the middle of paradise being chased by one! The two Ians couldn't stop laughing although I found it slightly less funny!

Carl Cox Motorsport has been getting into drag racing in quite a major way, and I don't mean me popping on a wig and a pair of high heels, I mean big, fuck-off engines and driving so fast that you need two parachutes to pop out the back to slow you down. I first had a go at drag racing for a bit of fun. Once you try it, it is basically the crack-cocaine of motorsports. It is incredibly addictive, and you just want to better yourself more and more as you look for that perfect 'high'. This is driving to a whole new level and, if you do it well, you can attain a level of concentration that most people will never reach. When I first wanted to get into this, I was conscious that, being a big guy, there might be limitations. Speaking to people in the industry, I asked them what you need to succeed at this. The answer from all of them was the same - you need a big pair of balls. Clearly, I was well suited for this!

As I write this my biggest achievement so far in any form of motorsport has been in this area and happened in January 2020. I managed to drive a quarter of a mile in 6.1 seconds, hitting a top speed of 234 miles per hour. When it came time to put my foot on the brake, I had my foot flat down to floor - and that's not just an expression. I was pumping the brakes like mad and the car was skidding. The reason for this was not because my beautiful 1967 Mustang, Eleanor, with enough engine power to get me to the moon and back, was not well put together, but because only one of the two parachutes had deployed. But I had done it. I had achieved a speed level that put me at the highest international level, and if I hadn't had to miss key qualifying events due to my DJ schedule, I would now be on the world stage competing at the highest level.

I'd actually only been at 70 per cent throttle for most of the drive. I'd started as typical Coxy, giving it 100 per cent, but the sheer power made me take my foot off a little. This car was a massive step-up from a conventional road car and I had to respect what I was doing and where my limits might be at that point. This is definitely something that I want to do in the future and my next goal is to break the 6-second mark and be able to get out of the car to tell the tale.

Owning a car like this is about as far away as you could be from my original Matchbox toy-car collection. I've always enjoyed going back to a time when motoring was stylish, and in my collection I have a Mustang, a Plymouth Road Runner and a 1964 Corvette. Doing what I do, I get invited to some amazing things and one of the highlights of the year for me is the Goodwood Revival. It's like going back in time with the old 1960s police cars, telephone boxes and the music that goes with it. I like dressing up; the nice tailored three-piece tweed suit with a flat cap is a nice change from my usual get-up. I was telling this to a guy who half an hour earlier had been dancing behind the decks when I played B2B with Fatboy Slim in London in 2019. Cars had come up in the conversation and suddenly he let me know that he's the chairman of the London Motor Show and asked me if I'd like to get involved. At first I thought he was inviting me down personally, and of course I would have said yes, but what developed through our shared support of the industry was that Carl Cox Motorsport has become showcased by the LMS. It's a proud moment for me and a testament to the hard work that everyone in the team puts into it.

Racing driving and DJing are not so dissimilar. To do both of them well requires hard work and determination. To do them really well requires those things plus skill and passion. To excel at them takes all those things I've just mentioned and also needs luck and opportunity. Like most things, it really is a case of being in the right place at the right time. Now that I'm fully immersed in the motorsport world, I don't ever see myself being out of it, and the pleasure I get from it means that I will be involved in this forever.

15.

In the Mix

Once upon a time, things were simple. A traditional DJ would just play other people's records and a typical producer would produce artists that the DJs would then play. This whole process involved major record labels, advertising campaigns, retailers and, of course, bands. Nobody knew that there was anything different or better because that was just the way things were.

Electronic music would change all of this. It would change it for the artists, it would change it for the industry, it would change it for big business and it would create opportunities for individuals in a way that had never happened before. Musically, you now had the power to control your output and to control your destiny.

I remember the first house record I played and that was in 1986, when I played 'Time to Jack' by Chip E., which is ironic as I was working for a carpenter at the time! I would say that this record was the beginning of the dance music movement in the UK. It changed everything. I would play this and it would literally stop the dancefloor dead. Most of my music back then was soulful and people didn't understand why I was playing a record that was clearly made on a machine and had no band playing the instruments. To me, the fact that this was created electronically was exciting and I felt like I was listening to the future. Music like this had no boundaries and I felt that this could be my entry into the music industry. At this point, house music came to the UK from the USA on import, so I'd be hunting for these records so that I could play them. Even though I only saw my path as a DJ, looking back, I think this is the moment when Carl Cox the producer was conceived. When I released 'I Want You (Forever)', it was part of a five-year deal with Perfecto to produce music. It was difficult because they thought I had the potential to be a pop star and so wanted more pop music that could be aligned with the rave scene, while I was already moving away from the commercial end of dance music. My second release for them, 'The Planet of Love', was good but not great. We both agreed that we didn't like the third record and they ditched me, which was a blessing in disguise.

My first label was called MMR, which stood for Most Music Records. It fell under the wing of Edel Records when they came to the UK from Germany. The dance music side was distributed by Flying Records in the UK from 1993 after the Italian Flying Records label set up a base here. As part of this, MMR became Ultimatum Music; they allowed me to have control over my sound and that's how I came to release my first album, *Enter the Cliché*. Rachel Turner had been tasked with setting up the UK arm of Flying Records and we hit it off right away. She really understood what I was trying to achieve and worked hard so I could deliver exactly the sound I wanted without having to go too commercial. I think without good people around me who knew the business, I wouldn't have been able to do that.

The great thing about having your own label is that you can release music by other artists who drop into your radar and would otherwise probably remain undiscovered. I'm really proud that I released Josh Abrahams's album *The Satyricon*, and I still work with him today.

My next move was to launch Intec in 1998. Intec stands for International Techno Sounds and was the start of what I really wanted to put out - the sound of who I am. Within this, I set up Ultimate Breaks, which was intertwined with my Ultimate B.A.S.E. club, so I was showcasing my own artists at my own night. Intec is still going strong today and still releasing great music.

Every couple of years or so I get approaches to bring out a big banging commercial album, but while I might entertain the idea at some point it has to work for me and be all about the music. I like the word integrity and what it stands for and I always say that word to myself when I start a recording. I'm lucky that I've been able to stay true to my values musically and also to have commercial success, which shows me that people who listen to what I think of as good music stand with me. My 1995 album, *F.A.C.T.*, ended up selling over 250,000 copies, which is phenomenal for techno, and my 'Two Paintings and a Drum' EP broke the Top 30 in the UK in 1996. I feel my music continues to grow with me and that's due to the support from the people who buy it. My 2005 album, *Second Sign*, did really well for me all across Europe, even reaching No. 3 in Spain's national chart. *Gracias*. By the time I released *All Roads Lead to the Dancefloor* on Intec in 2011 I was able to utilise state-of-the-art self-updating USB technology.

In 2018 I launched another label, Awesome Soundwave, which I put together with Christopher Coe, aka Digital Primate. This label is different to most dance labels, as we set it up specifically for live electronic artists with the aim of giving them room to experiment and to connect with each other.

It's a label for artists who make and perform their music live. As I know, producing live music in front of an audience with no studio back-up means that not only do you need to have very strong musicality, but you also have to know how to work every piece of equipment and make sure that all your machinery is talking to each other and to the audience. The whole point of this label was so that Christopher and I could give live electronic artists an outlet that would understand them while creating a community of like-minded people. We can put these artists in front of an audience and at the same time help nurture incredible talent that can push us further as well. Basically, we are putting water in their well and they are filling up ours at the same time. With the experience that we have, we can help creatives stay creative and aid them in navigating the industry.

You used to need quite a lot of hardware to make up a studio, whereas now you mostly need software. This means you don't need as much space, and bedroom producers who can work their way around the latest innovations can do great things relatively easily. You can also share your ideas and music in real time through the internet, and sending digital files means you can collaborate with another bedroom studio on the other side of the world.

Even when you know what you're doing, there can be nasty surprises in store, like the time when I was sued for copyright infringement. I met a guy called Steve Mason, who'd been on British Forces radio in Germany, and we'd got to know each other a little bit. He was with a small independent label and had written a track called 'Shallow Grave'; he asked me if I'd do a remix for him. This was the mid-90s and I was playing at festivals like Glastonbury and getting offered remixes left, right and centre. I really liked this track and thought I could do something with it for him. Having listened to it a few times, I liked the spirit of the record but felt it needed a lot more, so I rewrote the entire thing myself, produced it myself with no ghost producers around me and didn't even sample any part of the original track. The only thing I took was that my version was in the same key as Steve's. I wasn't expecting anything to come of this and, like most things that I do, I just wanted to make something that made sense for me. I was very happy with the finished result and so was Steve. People heard about the remix and started to seek it out and, before I knew it, it was No. 1 in the dance charts and had become a big tune. It was great for me because people knew that I had done it and, most importantly, *I* knew that I had done it. I had no contract with Steve and didn't need one because we were, and still are, friendly.

I was bringing out my own album and wanted to feature it as something I was proud of. After all, it really was an original composition by me and even the 'Shallow Grave' vocal is my voice. But the record label that Steve was on said no. I couldn't believe it and asked them, 'Why not?' They told me they wanted to retain it, so they could put it on a compilation album they were doing. I tried to explain that they would be getting double-bubble, as it would be on both my album and their compilation, but they refused to let me license it.

Anyway, in 1996 I decided that I would create my own track that had the spirit of my remix - or, as the judge would later say, I 'copied' it. I created a track called 'Phoebus Apollo' using my remix - which, you'll remember, was 100 per cent an original composition by me - as the basis for a totally new track. This track was quite big, charted really well and also had a video release. It was played everywhere and, two years later, Pete Tong put it on a compilation album. Only at this point did the little independent label, that had actually gone bust, come after me. I just ignored them. I thought they were a bunch of chancers, and I couldn't believe they expected me to give them anything. Next thing I know there's a court date and lawyers and all sorts of things in the mix. They even brought in a musicologist to compare my track to 'Shallow Grave'. I really thought I'd won this because I had taken nothing out of the remix and the remix had nothing much in common with 'Shallow Grave'. Because I'd only remixed Steve's original track, it really only had the bare bones in it, even though there really were no bones to pick over. The court disagreed and, in the end, I have to go with their findings. And that was that the bass lines, while not the same, had a similar pattern. This cost me £25,000 – an expensive way to learn a lesson! It also showed me that there's truth in the saying: 'Where there's a hit, there's a writ.'

The best way to explain what I do is to explain how I feel. I feel like I have music running around inside my body and the only way to get it out of my system is to lay it down. Everything I do starts organically and everything I release has some emotion inside it.

The first thing I do is lay down the drums. I know a lot of people do things differently, but I like to start there. It doesn't mean the drums won't change, but I always feel that that is the foundation of what I'm doing. Next, I lay down the bass line and that's the bit that's going to speak to the dancefloor and connect me to them. I love the energy between two bass lines working together and I know that when I'm mixing records in front of an audience, it's the bass lines that will start to weave the magic. Stage three is thinking about the chords – this is what picks me up. I don't like monotone and I like to think that this is what will separate my track from any others.

When I play out, the energy is built around the transition – not in the drop. I could play hit records all day long and look out at a sea of mobile phones ready to film the inevitable drop, but I pride myself on being creative. If every record had a drop, there'd be no challenge and the sets would be boring. Equally bad, I would be bored. Lots of new DJs think that it's easy and just involves getting the crowd to jump up and down, which sadly is probably right, as people are becoming conditioned to wait for the drop. To me, this is very short-sighted and almost what you'd call a career-killer. The weight of what I've experienced on dancefloors and the reaction I get from audiences is why I play the way that I do and is probably why I am bigger now than I ever have been.

Being a producer means that I can work and work and work on a tune until I feel that it is perfect for me. In fact, I think that there's only one track that I would call the perfect piece of music, which means that it is unremixable, and that is Stevie Wonder's 'Pastime Paradise'. If you listen to it from beginning to end, you will see just how excellent that track is. It blends perfect musicality with an incredible depth of feeling. Coolio sampled it on his 'Gangsta's Paradise', but listen to Stevie for the real deal.

I've worked in amazing studios with amazing artists and every experience is totally different. Imagine going to work every day to find different colleagues in a different building doing a different job. That's what it is like going into a studio. My favourite experience to date has been working with Nile

Rodgers. Nile, of course, is a super-legend. From his band Chic to working with artists like Daft Punk, Madonna, David Bowie and Lady Gaga, he has written, produced or performed on records that have sold over 500 million units. I had an amazing two days in the studio with him in Australia. Let me tell you how this came about.

I was performing at Ultra in Miami in 2015 when my tour manager Ian whispered in my ear, 'Nile Rodgers is here.' I thought that was a bit odd, because there are always people around, and Ian would only interrupt me when I was playing if it was important. He then whispered, and by whispered, I mean shouted at full volume because I'm on stage, 'He's behind you!' I turned my head to see Nile Rodgers taking pictures of *me* DJing. After the set, we had a good chat and talked about some ideas, but like all things in the heat of the moment, I didn't expect it to come to anything. I then bumped into him in Ibiza, where he was doing a charity gig and he asked me to sign his guitar, which had been autographed by major musicians. I really didn't feel worthy.

The next stop on our 'we must stop meeting like this' journey was at Bestival, when we chatted about Australia and I told him I had a house in Melbourne. It wasn't long before he was on tour and arrived in Melbourne, and his security guys contacted me and asked if I'd have time for a quick chat with him. I went to his hotel and he was sitting in the foyer waiting for me. He greeted me with a 'Hey, Carl' and suggested that he come over to my place and we make a track together. I rocked back on my heels and just said: 'Whaaaat?' I couldn't believe it. The plan was that I would pick him up the next day and we'd head into the studio and see what we could come up with.

I didn't think my studio was good enough for him, so I called up a techno producer I know called Steve Ward, who has a great studio an hour outside Melbourne, and asked if it was OK if I brought Nile Rodgers over for a couple of days. I could almost hear him falling to the ground over the phone. The next morning, I drove over to the hotel and picked up Nile with his trusty guitar to drive him to Langwarrin out in the suburbs. On the way we spoke about music and I told him that his track, 'Dance, Dance, Dance (Yowsah, Yowsah, Yowsah)' was the first twelve-inch that I'd owned and I used to play the B-side out a lot, which was called 'São Paulo', which had a sort of jazz feel to it. I pretty much played that record to death. He found it really interesting that I had picked up on that track from his whole catalogue, because it's one that he was particularly proud of.

On the way, Nile told me stories about all the guys that he'd worked with. I hadn't realised that Luther Vandross had provided back-up vocals on 'Dance, Dance, Dance' and that he was working as a session vocalist at the time. He was telling me stories about Diana Ross, David Bowie and Steve Arrington while I was trying to concentrate on keeping my hands on the steering wheel instead of hugging him, because here I am, a kid from nowhere, driving with a musical god sitting next to me. At one point, I wasn't even sure if I was dreaming this; even now, it seems very surreal when I think about it.

We pulled up at Steve's place and I introduced Nile, former musical director at Abbey Road Studios, home of the Beatles, to Steve and his mum as we prepared to go into his home studio. His mum came over and told Nile that she used to roller-skate to his music and so, with the ice broken, we went into the studio, a very relaxing and laid-back place. After we had been offered a cup of tea by Steve's mum, she left us to it. We talked first and discussed a few ideas and I asked him what he wanted to do, and he had this idea that we would try and do some sort of 'beats versus guitar licks' thing.

Getting started is always the hardest thing but I've spent a lot of time in the studio and I know that it's all about being comfortable and being confident. Now, with Nile Rodgers looking right at you and knowing that he's worked with some of the greatest musicians of all time, you don't want to start off on the wrong foot. The thing to do is just to forget that he's Nile Rodgers and remember that, like me, he is here because he loves music. I suggested we just record the whole day in one take and then see what we ended up with; we could always work on it the next day. I told Nile to close his eyes and just play whatever he wanted. After all, as I explained to him, he is the King and what had turned me on to his style was 'São Paulo', which was all about feeling free. I would then add beats and rhythms on top. He started to play, and it was lick after lick after lick. It was like gold dust, and we recorded enough material to fill numerous albums. I was getting busy too. I started with a four-bar loop and then brought in an eight-bar loop and we really created something special. We actually worked solidly for ten hours before I drove him back to his hotel with a plan to pick him up the next day.

I was absolutely buzzing. We had a good drive back and had spent all that time talking about music. Normally, after a long session in the studio I like to clear my head, especially if I'm going back in the next day. But what I did instead was, after dropping Nile off I turned right around and drove another hour and twenty minutes straight back to the studio and started working on the track. I worked right through until I'd finished it. Then I drove another hour or so back home.

The next morning, after no sleep, I picked Nile up, pushed the button and played the music in the car. He was absolutely stunned, which was the desired effect. I wanted to show him that I don't mess around. He was such a joy to work with and I really felt that I was not worthy, because he is someone who can work with anyone he wants. He liked the track – 'Ohh Baby'– so we actually put it out in 2016 as Carl Cox and Nile Rodgers. We had great chemistry, which is something that you can't manufacture. Being in a studio, really letting everything out, shows you who you can work with and who you can't, and we definitely want to work together again.

I'm often torn between being a live artist and being a DJ. Much of what I do as a DJ is remixing and producing on the fly, as well as selecting the right tracks for the crowd at that moment. I admire the live electronic artists because it really is such hard work to perform and produce your own music almost from scratch, in front of an audience. There's a lot that can go wrong and, unlike a DJ, you can't suddenly throw down a tune to keep things going.

When I DJ, everything is live anyway. Nothing is planned, set up in advance or pre-programmed and having spent much of my time working three decks, my concentration levels are always very high. I did originally have a live band around me. In 1992, Carl Cox Concept was a live act and played at places like Planet of Love alongside the Prodigy. Nobody knew at this point which direction electronic music was going to go in and because I was dependent on the unlicensed rave scene, I felt I might need to become a traditional recording artist if the scene was quashed. But after a while I felt that I was putting so much into the live side of things that it was encroaching on my DJing, which I was still trying to perfect. The big rave audiences wanted to hear me DJ and the promoters wanted to sell lots of tickets, which they knew my name would do. I could feel that the live side wasn't for now and was quite happy to put it on the back burner.

It feels like the media need to pigeonhole everything. They need to put everything neatly in its correct envelope, as they see it. This just doesn't work with music. Music is like a liquid - you pour it over a table and it can run into any and every direction, and no matter how many times you repeat it you'll never recreate exactly the same pattern. Now imagine pouring that glass of water into an envelope - it just can't work. I am often labelled as a techno DJ but even in a full-on techno set some of the music I play is not techno at all. If I'm playing across several players and taking a drumbeat from one track, blending a couple of melodies, adding a bass from another track and then adjusting the levels and frequencies on all of them, I'm actually playing something that didn't exist before. I take all types of sounds and blend them together, and that's what makes it my music. I play music that makes people happy. Whether my set heads towards a dark place, or it's more uplifting and melodic, the core of what I do is based around great tracks. There has to be passion behind it, and energy, and an element of edge. Sound has an edge.

My DJ style is actually based on hip-hop mixing. I've always liked the idea of the hip-hop style when playing house music, utilising the cuts and blends of records. I like to chop in a tune as well as blend. That's where the energy comes from.

But before I go on I like to have five or ten minutes of solace. I like to think about where I want to take the crowd, even though I know that the crowd will decide where we go that night. I always get nervous; I don't know anyone who doesn't. This is not being nervous that I won't deliver, it's more like an excited nervousness because I am about to release music that is building up inside me. It's like I am about to open a pressure valve. I try to sneak a peek at the crowd a few minutes before I go on stage so I know what I am going into. From then on, those few minutes pass very quickly. By now I am totally in the zone and I don't think that anybody can hold me back - we're doing this. It's very important for me to see how the audience are reacting to whoever is on before me so I can come in and lift them from the very first beat on the very first record. No long drawn-out build-up, I go in Usain Bolt style. Game on!

My 2011 album, *All Roads Lead to the Dancefloor*, was recorded using musicians, so I felt this was the opportunity to take a live show on tour. The thing is, if I can't give something 100 per cent, I'd rather not do it at all; and with my global commitments, I couldn't see how a tour could work and how I could get these musicians to where they needed to be. This was one of the things that spring-boarded Awesome Soundwave, because I just love seeing electronic music played live - if you can't beat 'em, join 'em.

During the lockdown in 2020 I was very fortunate to be in Melbourne where my main studio is situated. It isn't exactly Abbey Road, but El Rancho has everything I need to make and produce music at the highest level while also recording my live streams from there. Christopher Coe lives nearby so we're able to work on multiple projects at the same time, with Christopher acting like a human bookmark letting me know where I'm up to and making sure that everything happens in the right order. Some of the standout productions included my remix of 'Pomegranate' for Deadmau5 and the Neptunes, composing the opening soundtrack to the DAZN football series *Club Ibiza*, which aired in 200 territories, and mixing the Awesome Soundwave catalogue to create an album featuring only live electronic artists. I sent some footage to my manager of me in the studio jamming and he asked me who the track was by. When I said it was me there was a big pause in the conversation and I could almost hear the cogs turning. Within a few days the video had been shared to a few select mobile phones and before I knew it we were being approached by labels asking to hear the album. At this point there was no album, but the idea of an album and then developing more music from there was taking shape in my mind. Playing the music in online meetings and talking through concepts was making this seem like a possibility and I was blown away when BMG signed me as an artist to a worldwide recording contract.

I make sure to put time in to learn how to get the best out of all the new technology and can see that, in the future, I will go out with my own live electronic experience, probably with some very interesting collaborators performing live alongside me and delivering a next-level live electronic show where people come for the music (and hopefully the visuals) and where Carl Cox the DJ is very much secondary to the performance.

16.

Fantastic! Fantastic!

Dance music is all about creating moments where you connect with people. Being a DJ is not like any other job in the world. Most people go to work - a DJ goes to play. No two shows are the same and there are some that really stand out, those points when you think, 'That was something else!' And as I am telling my story here it makes sense to share a few of them with you.

This book has lots of my special moments in it, from Space and Ultra to drag racing and *Top of the Pops*, but I think this is a good point to share some of the unique experiences that focusing on this book have brought back for me.

For instance, when I was stuck in prison on my eighteenth birthday, I could have never imagined that thirty-six years later I would be invited to DJ at the Houses of Parliament! When I had the opportunity to play there I just thought, *These are the people who tried to squash our scene to the ground, squish it like a bug, but they forgot that young people have a voice, that they need to be heard, and that the government has no choice but to allow us to be heard.*

I remember going down to Parliament after they made this lobby group called 'Rock the Vote' in 1996. Eddie Izzard was the face of that and I had actually been at the House of Commons already, doing my bit as someone young people could relate to, trying to persuade them to vote.

Playing at Parliament was incredible. To think that this was the highest level of the Establishment, the same one that had tried to destroy the rave scene and dance culture. I'd been invited to perform for a fundraiser called House the House for the charity LNADJ (Last Night a DJ Saved My Life) that support children in crisis throughout the world. I felt that I was playing respectfully but I was still giving it 100 per cent Carl Cox. It wasn't long before I had a couple of officials come over asking me to turn it down - story of my life.

One of my greatest moments was my fortieth birthday party. Lynn Cosgrave hired a club in London and booked Light of the World, one of my favourite jazz-funk bands. I really wanted this to be a great night out for friends, as we seemed to spend most of our time missing each other at gigs and not really enjoying each other's company like we used to. Laurent Garnier was going to play and so was Leeroy James, who was part of my original party crew from back in the day. I called John Digweed up but he told me he couldn't make it because he was playing at Norman Cook's party in Brighton. WTF!!

I'd been so busy that I hadn't heard about a massive party on my very own doorstep. I'd heard the rumours about the whole beach being handed over for some sort of rave, but in dance music rumours about gigs that then never happen are everywhere. I was living in Brighton and unbelievably had picked the same weekend for my party as Fatboy Slim's Big Beach Boutique. So here I was, a Brighton-based DJ, having my little birthday party in London while 250,000 people partied at the biggest event Brighton had ever seen and possibly the biggest dance music event ever. Norman Cook rocked the seafront and back in London I had a fantastic night, surrounded by friends, getting busy on the dancefloor and listening to the music I love. There's no doubt that Norman's party was bigger, but I'm pretty sure that, to me at least, mine was better.

Early in the summer of 2018 I was booked to play a one-of-a-kind two-hour outdoor set at the sixteenth-century Château de Chambord in the Loire Valley in France. The organisers are also filmmakers, so captured the set from multiple angles as well as from the air, which has allowed me to look back at it and see how splendid the place is. The crowd were really into it and playing in front of a castle gave the whole thing a real sense of occasion. The stream was massive and despite the big open space the set had an intimate feel to it. The French have always supported me and have been a big influence on the whole dance music scene. From way back when, there has been a thriving underground scene that has crossed over to the mainstream while nurturing the next generation of new talent. The contribution from across the Channel is often overlooked, but we're talking about the land of Jean-Michel Jarre and a place that has given us phenomenal talent like Laurent Garnier, Daft Punk, Air, David Guetta, Birdy Nam Nam, Cassius, DJ Snake, Martin Solveig and Bob Sinclar. As my favourite TV character, Del Boy, once said, 'Mange tout, Rodney, mange tout.'

A few years earlier, in 2012, I'd been asked to take part in a programme for Sky Arts, *First Love*, that allows people to do something they loved but were not known for. From an early age I was all about soul music, and my mother, despite not being wild about my choices, had always believed in me. When I said I wanted to be a famous DJ one day, even though she didn't really know what I meant, she encouraged me to go for my dreams. I guess she was just happy that I was looking to do something positive, as there was a point when she thought I was headed down the wrong path. What she'd have really liked - and I'd have quite fancied too - was for me to be a professional pianist. I'd had a few piano lessons but at that time I didn't have the discipline to learn something from scratch.

This project would give me the chance to live that dream, even just for a moment. Maestros of the acid jazz scene, the Brand New Heavies, were scheduled to play in Ibiza and we worked out that our dates would collide, so the plan was that I would play with these pioneers in front of an audience. Not electronic music, mind you, but an electronic keyboard. This wasn't quite what I had in mind - I'd imagined myself sitting in a studio with a piano and being filmed with lots of cuts and editing to make sure I got it right. I bought myself a basic keyboard and started getting to grips with the music. We decided that we would play 'I Wish' by Steve Wonder, because it's a song I know very well and it was a tune where we could really funk it up.

With my touring schedule I was finding it hard to get enough practice in and only got to rehearse with the Heavies earlier on the day itself. I could see Simon (Bartholomew) and Andrew (Levy) exchanging glances during practice and I hoped they weren't regretting allowing me to share the stage with them.

Two hours before we were due to get going, I really didn't feel that I knew the music well enough to play alongside them, but I was doing this as much for my mum as for me, and I couldn't let her down. They played first and then called me up onto the stage. When I look at the footage now, they look nervous; I think they were expecting a car crash. But we pulled it off! I got it on the day and even threw in a couple of unplanned solos. I knew my mum would appreciate it and when she saw it she was in tears. 'I knew you had it in you!' she said. Thanks, Mum.

It wasn't just because I played that my mum was proud, but because it showed everyone who'd doubted me that I had what it took to be a success. In the build-up to the last night of Space I was involved in a small documentary that looked at where I had come from and where I had ended up. As part of that I went back to our old home in Carshalton that Mum and Dad left when they moved back to Barbados. I left there with no qualifications at all and now I was coming back as someone who had 'made it'. The place looked the same, but I looked up at my little window that used to have music blasting out 24/7 and tried to reconcile this with my life now. Most of the people I'd known seemed to have died or moved on. But some of the old neighbours came out and it was great to connect with them. We'd been the only black family in the area, but everyone in our street had always stood together. I think the neighbours who were hugging me on my return still saw me as 'little Carl' who'd wash their car or cut their grass for a pound. This visit, especially around the emotional rollercoaster of the closing of Space, made me look at my life and understand what I had done. It made me see that playing those records in my parents' front room on my dad's stereo was my first dance music moment.

While I felt a great sense of achievement being there, knowing that my drive had got me to where I am today, it did make me very sad. It made me think about when we moved out, and having to move away from the area with my two sisters to make a fresh start. I basically left all my friends behind when I moved to Brighton and we all lost touch very quickly - I had to begin again and make new friends. Despite this, the decision to go and to get into music was the right one for me. I was always about the music, it was almost like it was a hobby that I supported while being a builder and decorator. Back then, DJs who made money were radio DJs for commercial stations and the chance of me getting a gig like that was less than zero. Funnily enough, it was the rave-scene promotions on pirate radio which really made me famous all across the country. Stations like Festival Radio in Brighton, LWR in south London and Kiss helped turn Carl Cox into the People's Choice. I'll never forget how lucky I am.

At the end of summer 2019 I popped into a school in Chiswick to be the DJ at a school disco. My long-time friends Lynn Cosgrave and Andy Needham have children at the school and the disco was a charity fundraiser. They organised a sound system and I played a couple of hours of the latest chart hits to a room full of ten-year-olds. The kids had a great time, burning off steam and going wild in the school hall without the risk of getting in trouble, while I had their parents and teachers crowding around the DJ set-up. The kids didn't know who I was but the grown-ups did. It was refreshing to be able to do this – taking me back to when I was a schoolboy and played in the dinner hall in breaktime.

Not all special moments are so private. In September 2018 I was invited to play at Stonehenge – yes, that's right, the real Stonehenge! I played a full back-to-back set with Paul Oakenfold right up against this ancient wonder of the world. And before you ask, it was legal, licensed and approved. The 5,000-year-old stones are a special place, a place so special and magical that it draws people to it from all over the world. Back in the rave days I'd dreamt of playing there, and a few people tried it but were always moved on. Even bands like the Rolling

Stones couldn't make it happen, so when I got the phone call from Alon Shulman asking me to join him and Paul at the Universe event he was staging there I thought that it was a nice idea but couldn't possibly get off the ground.

It turned out that he'd already put it all together and had kept it on the low-down until everything was secured. English Heritage, who run the place for the nation, were on board and had approved the plan, which involved electronic music and a full production that included lasers and mapping the stones, plus filming, including by drone. Alon's unique events are always special and he always has a surprise up his sleeve for the audience. In this case, the surprise was little old me! Of course, I wasn't going to pass this up and the plan was that I would fly over from Ibiza where I was performing and make my way to Stonehenge to join Paul after his set when we could play together.

When I got there on the big day there was a special feeling in the air as guests started arriving. Lots of the original acid house DJs had come to see this happen and Mark Moore, Danny Rampling, Nancy Noise, Terry Farley, Tintin from Energy, Mr. OZ and Carl Loben were in the crowd. Oakenfold had asked me specially to join him at Stonehenge, and that (nearly) makes up for him not including me at the opening of Spectrum! Paul choreographed his set to the sunset and created something very special by mixing the likes of Vangelis, William Orbit, Hans Zimmer and Empire of the Sun. Alon had managed to get permission for people to actually dance in the middle of the stone circle and I looked at that and thought how far we'd come from being chased through the countryside to now being official guests at what is one of the most important historic sites in the world.

I felt very proud as we played our music there, and the amazing energy of Stonehenge added to the occasion. Everyone was smiling, some were crying, and some were just lost in the music. We are all like-minded people and the music was bringing us closer together. To have a DJ booth to perform from there was amazing. Paul and I have very different styles but we both share a history and a love of all forms of music. We complemented each other, mixing different kinds of house and techno, an unplanned set where we just vibed off each other and the location. Our set was streamed and it was like New Year's Eve 1999, when I was able to share something important to me with dance music fans all over the planet. I closed our B2B set with Paul Rutherford's 1988 classic 'Get Real', which felt like the perfect end to a perfect day. A lot of people don't know that Rutherford, a member of Frankie Goes To Hollywood, who 'came to dance', created one of the most influential acid house tracks and was a regular at clubs like Shoom.

We'd pulled it off, and the next day the story was everywhere. Not just *DJ Mag*, *Mixmag* and *Rolling Stone*, but the *New York Times*, the *Guardian*, CNN worldwide and the BBC. The whole experience was incredibly special for me, not just because I was there or that I was sharing it with good friends, but because once again we were pushing dance music to the forefront of the kind of moments that it was originally created for. Unifying dancefloors, no matter where they are.

There have been so many amazing moments that I've been lucky to be part of and that I've been able to share or be included in. There isn't one that I could say is the best - especially as I believe the best is yet to come - and each is unique and so special for different reasons. There is, however, one moment that I think about a lot. It isn't really music-related, although I had provided a sound system, played some records and was surrounded by rock'n'roll history. It was when the Fab Four's Paul McCartney asked me to join him for a slice of pizza at Stella's eighteenth. At the time I felt it was a very significant moment for me, and all these years later I still feel a huge sense of pride that at that point in my life I had got myself into a position where something like that could happen to someone like me - and whenever I think about it, I can still taste the oregano.

17.

Cabin Fever

At the end of February 2020 I headlined the Electric Daisy Carnival show in Mexico before heading over to Los Angeles to kick off a US tour that would cover the whole country, including an even bigger Carl Cox Megastructure at Ultra in Miami, ending up in New York at the end of March. Then it would be on to the UK, where I'd be based throughout the summer while performing at festivals including Glastonbury and across Europe before a massive stand-alone London show at the end of September.

The first LA show was phenomenal and if the audience reaction was a taste of things to come I was in for a fantastic month. We were starting to hear about a virus in China but during my next two shows in Chicago and Denver my focus was 100 per cent on the music. Suddenly, Covid-19 became more than a remote news story as a global pandemic was declared. I still thought the tour would carry on, but as the situation worsened this was clearly not going to be. I spent hours on the phone with management, promoters and family while trying to second-guess what was likely to happen. Within a week I'd flown back home to Melbourne.

Australia went straight into a serious lockdown and I realised that I wouldn't be heading back to America any time soon.

The tour was rescheduled for October, but even with wishful thinking I could see by the level of government response that this was unlikely to happen. I'm not used to not being busy, and the first few days were the hardest. Not knowing what was going to happen and working out arrangements with promoters for new dates for the postponed shows amplified the problem.

My set-up in Australia is pretty cool. My home is a short drive from my studio so I decided that getting into the studio was what I should do. I started a little vegetable patch at home and began posting little videos of what I was up to. My banana bread was a big hit and it was while going through the comments that I realised I could play a set or two online for people to enjoy. I keep my music collection in Australia, so with 150,000 records in the house a vinyl set was the obvious choice. My *Cabin Fever* set was a lo-fi affair: just me in a pair of shorts and slippers playing tunes and chatting on the mic. Straight away I was being asked, 'When's the next *Cabin Fever?*' so I thought I'd better do another one. Before I knew it I was delivering a weekly show: *Cabin Fever – the Vinyl Sessions.*

As the lockdown rolled on, the shows became as important to me as they seemed to be to the audience. The concept is simple. I pull out a bunch of records based around a theme and play them on three turntables. House, techno and rave shows sit comfortably alongside funk, soul and disco sets. I also do specialist shows where I focus on a particular label like Bush or Soma, or play overlooked album tracks like the Prince-penned 'Yes' by The Family.

The most important *Cabin Fever*, and the most emotional set I've ever played, was the tribute to my father. I'd been to see my dad in Barbados in December 2019 before my Hawaii show, when things had looked bleak but he'd seemed to recover.

Sadly, he died on 1 July 2020; not being able to get out there because of the pandemic made this very hard. The funeral was streamed live on Facebook and seeing the open casket and my family and sisters there while I was stuck in Australia was very difficult. I decided that I would dedicate a special *Cabin Fever* to Henry Carlisle Cox and that I would play his actual records. I struggled to hold it together as I held those 45s, but the audience stayed with me as I played soul, disco and calypso. These were records I'd played in our front room as a little boy and were the foundations of my DJing career. My manager Alon somehow arranged for the Prime Minister of Barbados, Mia Mottley, to join me during the set on a live video call, which was an incredible honour for me and a special tribute to my father. I ended the show playing the full album version of Santana's 'Black Magic Woman', and as the stream came to an end the tears started to flow.

It's important to me that *Cabin Fever* can be enjoyed by everyone, so I decided from the start that it would be a free-to-view show. People can enjoy it live every week and it can be found on various platforms. I chose to create an audio-only archive and have that sitting in my Mixcloud Select, where subscribers can listen to all the shows online and offline whenever they want, knowing that the platform pays all the labels of the tracks I play and therefore the musicians and artists also get paid. I've spent years buying records and this is my way of curating and sharing the ownership of my collection. I love the thought that I'm passing on my collection to music lovers everywhere. The icing on the cake was *Carl Cox's Cabin Fever* winning Best Solo Stream Series at the *DJ Mag* Best of British Awards, voted for by the public.

Looking at social media, it's easy to see why the pandemic was about more than just a virus. People were sat at home in front of screens and social media gave them a voice and a platform to share that voice. Suddenly everyone seemed to be a scientist, activist and a politician. Lockdowns, masks, BLM and Trump were some of the topics that divided friends. Then we moved on to vote-rigging, vaccinations and getting clubbing going again. I try to stay back from most of the heated debates but I wade in if I feel I can add something. I was doing a Q&A as part of the virtual Brighton Music Conference in October after the UK government were telling people in the arts to retrain and that only viable industries would be supported. I felt that I needed to speak up, and said that was totally wrong, we *are* viable. Even before the Q&A was over this made the lead news story on *DJ Mag*. Even before you consider the financial contribution from the dance music industry, the creative and cultural side alone is worth saving.

I couldn't go out and perform but was in the studio every day working on new music, remixes and virtual shows. I was doing at least two shows per week. Playing 'trackside' live from Melbourne at the McLaren party in the UK for the seventieth anniversary of Silverstone was a lot of fun and the next best thing to being there. Aside from *Cabin Fever*, my alter ego Pablo Hassan did a *Human Traffic* set and I played for some really great causes, including Nicole Moudaber's show in support of those caught up in the explosion in Beirut, Last Night A DJ Saved My Life, and a special set for London's Evelina Children's Hospital.

New Year's Eve 2020 was the perfect opportunity to share my passion for music and try to create a few smiles along the way. NYE parties were pretty much cancelled across the globe, often alongside national lockdowns. Going live on NYE takes some planning to make sure that the connections are in place and that you don't mess up the all-important count-down. Fortunately, the restrictions were eased in Melbourne so I was able to be in the studio and enjoy the evening with a few people. I kicked off with midnight in Melbourne for the Beatport 21-hour show, which included Nicole Moudaber in Barbados, Jamie Jones in Miami, DJ BLT in New Delhi and Honey Dijon in Berlin. The show went around the globe, ending up back with me the following evening in Melbourne. Because of the time difference I was also able to perform as Pablo Hassan for a special set at midnight in the UK, which was free to view and great fun to do. To crown the night off I had pre-recorded a special mix for Apple, which also went out for New Year's Eve. It also gave me the opportunity to reflect on the year we had just experienced and to realise just how fortunate so many of us are. I definitely stepped into 2021 putting my best foot forward, straight back into the studio.

Not touring, and in particular not travelling, meant that I could really focus on my studio work. I was already collab-orating on AI and VR projects for 2022, but my newfound lockdown freedom allowed me to catch up with my remix and production side and to try out new things. The remix of 'Pomegranate' for Deadmau5 and the Neptunes had more of a pop edge than I usually deliver, but I really enjoyed doing it and it went down amazingly well.

Spending so much time in the studio and collaborating with Christopher Coe, my partner at Awesome Soundwave, led me to explore my live side. I felt that I had something special, but with no audience to play for it was hard to see if my original compositions played live would work. I hit on the idea of making a couple of my virtual DJ sets into live performances, starting with the Mysteryland show. The reception was off the scale, and working on new material, including my album and live show, kept me sane during what turned into the most difficult year of my life. Although losing my father during a global pandemic was almost unimaginable, I was very conscious that everyone on the planet was suffering in some way. The daily news became more and more heartbreaking and it was clear that this was the time for us all to give each other emotional support where possible.

But an amazing thing did happen in January 2021. Melbourne had endured one of the harshest anti-Covid-19 lockdowns on the planet in 2020 and the people had rallied to support it, meaning that, by the new year, cases were almost non-existent. January is summertime in Australia, so the weather is excellent and, with the drop in cases and the city opening up, we felt that it would be possible to have a party. I made my name in the days of the unlicensed rave scene in the UK but with the pandemic I was strongly of the belief that doing anything like that would be selfish and dangerous. With clear social distancing and safety guidelines in place, I was able to hold two parties for a sell-out crowd of 3,000 people per event. Carl and Eric's Mobile Disco took place in a roofless stadium and it was amazing. While nearly all the world's entertainment venues were closed and with the majority of physical events for the foreseeable future cancelled, we staged a legal and licensed show. People danced and laughed, and so did we. Eric Powell had on a particularly festive Hawaiian shirt and I also went all out. It was wonderful to play to such an up-for-it crowd, who had been waiting for almost a year to bust some moves. By contrast, I'd been on the phone to my manager in London just before I went on and he was building a snowman with his kids in his garden under a nationwide lockdown. This made me realise just how lucky I was and how much respect and admiration I have for the people of Melbourne.

18.

Mind, Body and Soul

We are one. We came together to dance and, on the way, got to know each other really well. We broke down barriers and opened doors so, no matter who you are, your race, your colour, your gender and nationality, you can come together and party. We learned a lot about each other: how to behave, how to help each other and how fragile we can be.

Mental health has become a talking point in the dance music community, something that we want to understand, that affects people who need our support. People are starting to understand that seeking help is not a bad thing, and it is amazing how many people I know who have tried to reach out in the last couple of years, sometimes personally but often publicly through social media. But it's the ones who don't reach out but who desperately need help that we need to look out for the most. Sadly, some people fall through the cracks and, before we realise how much help they need, it is too late.

This was the case with Tim Burgling, who took his own life in April 2018 at the young age of twenty-eight. He'd been a DJ since he was sixteen and, very quickly, this young Swedish guy became a global superstar. He was Tim to his parents, but we all got to know him as Avicii. In his relatively short life, he topped the charts around the world, was nominated for a

Grammy Award and played to sell-out crowds everywhere. He was a lovely guy who seemed to have it all, but clearly struggled with the huge pressure to keep going and not disappoint his fans and record label. His constant touring and endless commitments in the studio were taking their toll and for the last couple of years he had withdrawn from many gigs. Having started so young and being catapulted straight away to the highest level meant he hadn't built up the kind of support network you need to ground you when you're not on stage. His death was a major wake-up call to artists, management, bookers and the media and is still sending shock waves round the industry.

I couldn't start talking about mental health without mentioning Avicii, who showed us the best and the worst sides of the dance music industry. I've been around a long time and have seen a lot, and I can see that the pressure of constantly touring, travelling and always having to be switched on with a big smile can have a heavy impact, however positive or otherwise your outlook is. I've been very lucky. From the start, I was always surrounded with good friends; as my career took off, these friends always made sure that as well as thinking of the audiences and the fans, I'm also thinking about myself. I always make sure to find some 'Carl time' where I can sit back and reflect on what I'm doing and what I want to be doing.

I always feel super-lucky to do what I do. I could not wish for a better life than the one I lead. I have countless friends across the world and, by friends, I mean people who share my values and who if I bumped into them would welcome me with a smile. Life isn't always easy but it's important to be able to recognise when you're struggling a bit or need a bit of a time-out. There are lonely times and sometimes a bit too much space to think about things.

Conversely, being switched on 24/7 can be exhausting and sometimes a little too much. There's nothing worse than stepping off a transatlantic flight waiting for your luggage, only to have a smartphone pushed in your face with someone saying: 'Do you mind if I take a selfie with you?' And when it happens about fifty times in the space of about a ten-minute period it can get a bit much. But then I always remember the reason they want my picture, and that's because they know who I am and what I do and I have touched them in some way. I think I'd be a lot more worried if they *didn't* want my picture; that constant attention is part of the life. Technology means that people can take your picture and release it to the world in an instant, but it also means that I can release my music and my message to the world in an instant too. This is what you might call a 'first-world' problem. But I'm on this ride till the end, so I need to enjoy every moment as best I can.

At first I was really shocked by Avicii's tragedy, but the more I thought about it and spoke to other DJs, the less shocking it became. I think I was more surprised that Avicii didn't seem to have felt he had anywhere to turn and saw suicide as the only way out. When really talented people like Prince and David Bowie pass on unexpectedly we all feel saddened and collectively mourn their loss with shared memories while looking back at their legacy; but to take your own life so young when you clearly have so much talent and so much more to give is staggering. Speaking to good friends in the industry, it became clear that a lot of people out there are struggling. Suicide is one of the biggest killers among young men and I hear that sometimes things can spiral quickly. There are lots of great organisations out there that can give advice and support, and lots of like-minded people who'll understand, so don't hesitate to reach out for yourself or a friend if you think it's needed.

Even when things seem bleak there is often something good around the corner and with hindsight we can see that what seemed a major setback was just a blip. The hard part is getting round that corner so you can have the luxury of looking back. I'm sitting here at El Rancho, my custom-built studio at the farm in Melbourne, reading this through. I'm surrounded by sound equipment and awards – the tools of my trade and the accolades I've received for doing a good job. In the middle of the trophy shelf is a piece of perspex and inside it is a 50-pence piece. I have it there to remind me of what was literally one of my darkest times.

Back in the mid-80s, when I had just moved to Brighton and was looking after my sisters, we used to have an electricity meter. I was OK at budgeting, making sure we had rent money, food, heat and electricity, but had been playing a few tracks too many and we'd run out of electricity. This meant no hot water, no heat, no cooking, no TV, no light and – worst of all – no music. Between us we couldn't even scrape together 50p for the electricity meter to get the lights back on, so it was an early night for the girls. I felt like such a failure, I was supposed to be a man and I didn't even have 50p to my name. Even though I knew it would only be for one night and that I could earn the next day, I sank very low very quickly. It was such a quick descent and I could see how easy it would be to slip over the edge. This scared me more than anything. I sat on the sofa all night, staring out of the window and waiting for the sun to come up so that I could get out there and start grafting. I was determined that we would never go without again.

Walking from my living room to the studio, I passed four-teen light switches, all of which had been left on. I switched them off. It was like I was looking at the trappings of my success on the way to the 50p coin to remind me that every coin has two sides and how fine the line can be between it landing heads or tails. I'm not showing off by saying what I have now – you'd have to have come from where I have and struggled like I did to know that this is not showing off but pride in my achievements. Everything I have has come to me through hard work; I had nothing on a plate. I earned it.

As Avicii has shown, you can have everything but still feel like you have nothing. The death that hit me the hardest was Keith Flint's in 2019. I'd known Keith from the earliest rave days. He was a frenzied dancer who could go for hours. Him and his mate Leeroy Thornhill danced on stage while Liam Howlett played his music and MC Maxim added live vocals to get the rave crowd going. The energetic stage show and Liam's electronic genius made the Prodigy one of the greatest, if not *the* greatest, live dance music acts. In 1996 Keith, now with his trademark hair style, became the frontman and vocalist and 'Firestarter' smashed its way into our cultural history.

Like me, Keith was into his bikes and also owned a racing team, Team Traction Control. His team were right up there, winning three Isle of Man TT races in 2015. We had lots of good times around bikes and I think people were surprised to see Keith and Coxy in our leathers, leaning against bikes beside a racetrack. We'd both made our names on the rave scene and here we were, racing-team owners. Prodigy were touring around the world and had a new album out and were rumoured to be going to play Glastonbury in summer 2019 – it seemed that life couldn't be sweeter for him. He was always a real laugh, good fun to be around, but I knew that being so recognisable wasn't something he enjoyed. I played 'Firestarter' in many of my sets that year after his death in March, but it was no consolation. It was as if his passing had sucked a little of the energy out of the track. I still miss Keith today.

I've always been safe in the knowledge that I have good friends and family to fall back on when I need a cushion. I'm not a small guy by any stretch of the imagination, but I know that no matter how hard I fall emotionally someone will be there to catch me. Even in my darkest times, like after the Venezuela gig or the death of my beloved mother, I have been picked up and carried through by the people around me.

Nothing has had a worse effect on the industry than the Covid-19 pandemic. The important thing to remember is that you are not alone. You might think these are just empty words, but it's true – even if you think you are you don't need to be. We are a community and it's OK to ask for help. It's also OK to ask somebody if they want some help. Things are not always what they seem. Sometimes the most popular person in the centre of the busiest room can be the loneliest person on Earth, while 'Norman no mates' sitting in the corner alone might be perfectly happy.

As you can tell, I'm a happy guy. I have great friends, a great life and I love living life to the full. Hopefully, anyone on my dancefloor can feel the love and no one should suffer in silence or be alone. As we move headfirst into the roaring twenties we should go forward with the motto: 'No one left behind'.

19.

Oh Yes, Oh Yes!

People often come up to me and say, 'What's the plan?' because
I have so much going on they think that everything must be
super-organised and that I must be ticking things off a list and
working through some sort of formula. The reality is that there
is no formula. I never had a plan and every time I thought I did,
I didn't stick to it. Life is a series of moments that you either
connect for yourself or are connected for you. How you deal
with these moments and how they affect you is just a part of
the journey you are on.

Being where I am now, I can say that I will be hands-on
in music and motorsport for ever. Having a studio and a label
means that I will always be involved in music - everything
from performing and producing to remixing and writing. In
the early days, I was just desperate to get a booking, whereas
now I'm also creating and programming festivals and events.
This means that as well as always having a platform that I'm
happy to play on, I'm able to bring forward and showcase new
and interesting talent. Having rediscovered my live-artist side
I will be focusing on my own music in the studio. I feel that
I really stand for something and, through hard work, am an
integral part of every aspect of dance music. I can't see myself
ever retiring.

There have been two times in my career where I nearly retired. The first time was in 1993 and I was in Manchester with Justin Berkmann from Ministry of Sound. I was thirty, I was playing everywhere and getting very tired, and just thought to myself that maybe it was time to call it a day. A couple of days later, I was at Cream in Liverpool and could see that what I had been a big part of creating - global dance culture - was bigger than ever and would keep growing and growing. I thought to myself, *How can I walk away from and turn my back on this?* The second time I nearly retired was, as you know, over the whole Venezuela thing; again, it was a brief lapse of focus due to circumstances way beyond my control.

I really don't feel that as a creative I can retire, because instead of retiring it would be quitting and throwing away everything that I have worked for. And I ain't no quitter. I never forget how lucky I've been. Lucky that there is a lot of interest in what I do and that whatever I want to do is in my own hands.

There's a lot to be said for being in the right place at the right time as part of a path of success. Thirty years ago, if you told people you were a DJ, they would ask you which radio station you were on. If you told them you wanted to be a DJ in clubs, they would laugh at you and tell you to go and get a proper job. The whole club scene as we know it came out of DJs who were not on the radio and were playing music that most people had never heard before. The only radio that was useful to me was pirate radio, like Centreforce and Kiss, because they would be used by the rave promoters to get people to know about the parties and so help get my name out there. Before the likes of Radio 1 started to champion dance music, we never had the power that mainstream radio brings to get our music heard. Today, the internet has changed everything. The latest generation of DJs have it easy. They don't have to carry record boxes and make the effort to get to know the players on the almost-invisible underground scene. For some of these DJs, the only hard work they are doing is reposting from Facebook to Instagram, and that's how they get their bookings. Popularity is judged more by likes and shares that it is by praise for achievement. I read the other day a post from a guy who said he was 'old school' and was taking a break, having been DJing for a whole five years!

Don't get me wrong, the future is bright, with some incredible artists coming through, but people have to be careful and not panic if they don't get the attention they crave after five minutes. A good friend of mine was upset that no one wished him a happy birthday on Facebook – then he realised that his privacy settings blocked the date from being revealed! He's not even that into social media but says he felt genuinely distressed. The best way to earn your stripes is through integrity and if there isn't enough water in the well, people won't come and drink.

One of the best things about the scene is that it rejuvenates itself and self-propels into another era. It's like a relay of life, but instead of the runner dropping out when they pass you the baton, they keep running with you, and we are now a stampede that cannot be turned back. I was there at the starting blocks, at the beginning of this race when there were only a few of us lined up together. Nobody thought we would get to the point where we could control things musically and also turn this into a business. In the same way that we found inspiration from everything around us, the evolving scene keeps adding more and more layers as more people want to be part of it. What was seen as an underground counterculture by the Establishment is now used to motivate the next generation. Dance music was always about being all inclusive and breaking down all boundaries.

Originally, the majority of DJs and producers were male, but girls were hearing the same music and being exposed to the same things, so it was inevitable that this would change. I remember when you'd struggle to name more than a handful of female DJs. You'd probably come up with DJ Rap, Lisa Loud, Monika Kruse, Nancy Noise and Gayle San, and then probably struggle to come up with many more unless you were really into the scene. Nowadays, the industry is filled with female artists performing at the highest level. World-class DJs like Charlotte de Witte, Anna, Nicole Moudaber and Amelie Lens have inspired thousands of girls who could never have imagined being a DJ to want to come through. Any colour, any race, any genre, any nationality, any gender – all are welcome. These are fantastic times and I feel that we are opening the doors to the future. I still worry about the culture and where we are, but the important thing is that it is growing and going in the right direction – forwards.

I think my advice to the new breed of DJs is to take your time. If you're hot, you're hot. If you're not, and you've had some sort of stroke of luck, then you're probably on a one-year cycle and that will be it. So really, you should focus on doing what you believe and letting the music be your reward. It's all about sticking to your path and never giving up. You can always find a piece of music that will motivate you and keep you following your destiny. Mine is 'Can You Get It' by Mandrill from their *We Are One* album, the kind of track that I will be dancing to for ever and ever.

I love the future but I do like to look back, with a bit of nostalgia, at where we came from. There was a lot more camaraderie in the past among the DJs and we had a lot of interaction with the clubbers, many of whom became our friends. You'd go to an event and it was basically a mystery party. When you got to the party, you played your set and stayed through until the end. All the DJs supported each other, and we were working to make things work for all of us. These days it's all set up for you. You turn up and do what you've got to do, which is a far cry from the days when we had to be all over it from beginning to end. I can't help but miss the pioneering days when you'd get into a car looking for the rave and almost always get lost, making a few friends on the way and then finally get to the party. Back then, you'd play your set, hug it out and enjoy the party. I guess the key thing is that everyone wants to enjoy the party, so we're not so different today - after all, who doesn't want to enjoy a party?

It's funny to think that when this whole movement started Paul Oakenfold named his club night 'Future'. It was the first club that called itself Balearic and to make sure the people got the message he actually put on the flyers, 'The Original and Only Balearic Club - Dance, You Fuckers'. He called it Future because at the time it seemed that we had stumbled upon the very essence of what the future would be. Thirty years on, I'm actually in our future. And it's not very different from what I imagined. Sure, there are lots of new technologies and things we should and shouldn't do, and the political landscape is a mess on a good day and a disaster on most. But that's not what we're about - we're all about bringing people together and uniting everyone, and that is what I think we have done. You can be into anything or nothing and be into everyone or no one and still be part of what's going on. There's no such thing as the cool kids any more; we're all cool, but only if we wanna be. Sometimes it's just cooler not to be cool.

The thing that has brought us all together is one word. Music. It doesn't matter if it comes from Detroit or Manchester and it doesn't matter if it's made in a studio or in your bedroom - music has managed to touch our very souls and helped us break open doors, given us the freedom to be or do anything we want. If it wasn't for music I wouldn't be who I am.

The newest dance music sound is anchored in what we were doing when the whole scene started and it makes me feel good when I play a festival with a mixed line-up to know that I'm one of the originators of what people are listening to now. It's crazy to think that it's still going on today, stronger than we could have imagined, and that makes me really happy. The craziest thing of all is that, with all the evolving and new genres and then the EDM explosion into the pop charts, techno is bigger than ever.

The rise of EDM has played a big part in techno staying so strong. The EDM sets are all about the big hits and there are only so many times that people, even real EDMers, want to hear the same tunes at an event. Techno takes you on a different kind of journey. You're still dancing, but listening out for the unexpected, and it is that unexpectedness that makes it so different and so special. You don't need to be 'main-stage ready' and can rock a basement of 200 people just as well as a big festival crowd. I like to think that as the EDM audience grows up and is replaced by a new generation, the previous one moves into a different electronic music experience. Techno is always ready and waiting for anyone who wants to jump in, it's not going anywhere.

As dance music has grown to become, in my opinion, the leading cultural movement on the planet it has opened up amazing possibilities and opportunities for all involved. It was initially looked at with suspicion; I remember in the early 90s trying to get a little bit of a sponsorship for a party from a drinks company who said that this wasn't for them as they wanted to appeal to the youth market in a big way. I remember thinking, *If thousands of young people who want to drink it isn't for you, then what is?* Where we are today is that people who run brands can make a difference and they understand where dance music has come from and the power it has. The people running these brands were probably clubbers themselves; and when I say 'were', I really mean 'are'. Now, instead of us chasing the brands, they are chasing us. The key thing is to only work with companies that can help take things further for the whole scene. It's not about sticking logos on everything but about the sponsor becoming a partner and adding value in different ways.

At the beginning there wasn't a single brand that wanted to work with me, and I guess that's one of the reasons that now I really have to believe in a collaboration to take part in it. One of the recent collaborations I am most proud of is my partnership with the watch brand Zenith, which started in 2020. Over the years they have had very few partnerships themselves, most recently with Felix Baumgartner, who in 2012 jumped to Earth out of a helium balloon from the stratosphere, reaching a top speed of over 840 miles per hour, and rock legends the Rolling Stones. I was amazed when they approached me. I helped design the Carl Cox timepiece, which has a cog in it resembling a vinyl record. They've also started to get behind some of the live electronic things that we're doing with our artists at Awesome Soundwave and there's even a twelve-inch in the watch case. I feel very proud of this, firstly because it shows me how far dance music has come that a luxury brand like this can recognise our industry and secondly, on a personal level, it shows me that my unswerving passion for what I do and the way that I do it is recognised by a company like this. This is on my wrist alongside my Carl Cox/Electric Family bracelet, which helps raise money for an education project in Kenya that I support and that Jim Mason, my old scaffolding boss, helps to run.

Recognition is a good feeling if you get it for the right reasons. It took me a long time to be recognised for the thing I wanted to be known for, which was music. I've seen some talented young people who have broken through much earlier like Martin Garrix has done. The singer Billie Eilish shows that talent is talent and some people just have it. In 2020, aged just eighteen, she scooped five Grammy Awards and is part of a new generation of artists that have the opportunity to connect with you on a very personal level. The generation that listen to her are streaming from their phones to their brains via earphones and so she literally gets inside their heads.

Music being so accessible these days means that artists who may have been frozen out by traditional major labels can now get heard. You only need someone wanting to make the music and someone wanting to listen to it to make this happen. Word of mouth has moved online but means that music gets shared quickly. You just need to give the unknown a chance, which is easier now that music can be reached at the touch of a button. I kicked off my monthly residency on Radio 1 in the spring of 2021, which means I can share fantastic new music that comes onto my radar from emerging electronic artists.

Obviously, pre-internet you had to search out music from record shops and through friends, and as a DJ I'd also receive promos and white labels to listen to. It was a trade-off – we'd get free tunes, the latest stuff, and they'd get to see how the DJs reacted to it. Back in 1992, in the very early days of the super-big raves, I was playing at Amnesia House up in the Midlands. It was a massive event and the Prodigy were playing live too. The party has become known as 'The Rave Wedding' because the promoter actually got married on stage during the event and advertised it on the flyer as if that was an attraction. Nick Halkes from XL Recordings was standing on the side of the stage – they had the Prodigy on their label – and I was playing as he came over to say hi. He had a record with him and I asked if that was for me. He said, 'It's the new Kicks Like A Mule joint', which was an act he was also in. He asked me if I wanted to have a listen, so I pulled it out from under his arm, dropped the sleeve on the floor and put it on my third turntable. It turned out it was the acetate, the test copy you master in the studio before you press up the vinyl. Didn't bother me. I dipped the needle across the track to get a measure of it and it sounded good, it gave me a buzz. To Nick's surprise, I mixed the track straight in with what I was playing and the crowd loved it. He'd meant for me to listen to it after my set. With me, it was always about hearing new music, and this track had my radar up straight away, so I figured if I got it then so would the crowd. When you know, you know.

Electronic music is much more than just a type of music or a genre or even a culture. It is a feeling, which is why it gets stronger and stronger. There's something new every day, and I want to be part of it. I love all of it so much. I can't imagine what new things will cross my path next week, let alone know what I'll be doing in the distant future. Sometimes I wish I knew what would happen but mostly I like the surprise. Underground becomes mainstream and mainstream becomes underground. There is no right or wrong. The music simply evolves, so a bit of the future is already with us. I like to think that all dance music is the sound of Now!

From struggling to buy a sandwich to being able to walk into any restaurant in the world and have a meal is all down to what I do. I've got a lot to show for my success, but I honestly believe that the fruits of my labour is seeing those smiles on the dancefloor. That's all I ever wanted from life and that is what I've got.

Afterword

BY JOHN DIGWEED

There are DJs, then there are the DJs' DJs, and then there is the one and only Carl Cox.

Carl has been a giant in the dance music world since the explosion of the acid house scene back in 1987. I knew Carl before this and even back then he was a giant. I must have met him around 1985; I was playing mostly in Hastings but the club I worked for had venues in Brighton, which had a much more vibrant club scene, and Carl was already one of the key DJs in the city. I managed to get on some gigs playing alongside Carl at venues like the Zap, Club Savannah and the Escape, as well as raves like Storm and Passion. From my first meetings with Carl I was struck by how friendly and down-to-earth he was, with no ego at all. He was also incredibly hard-working. He had maybe two or three gigs a night during the weekend and he also had his own sound system that he would be taking round and setting up at venues and then collecting during the early hours, ready for the next day. You could see his passion for music and the scene. Even with the incredibly long hours he always had time for everyone, greeting them with that massive smile on his face.

He has always been a man of the people and the energy he emits as soon as he enters the DJ booth and the crowd's reaction to him - today as much as ever - shows the love there is for Carl and for his craft and passion. When I started the first Bedrock parties in Hastings back in 1990 Carl was so helpful to me and was almost a semi-resident, playing at many of those first parties at the Crypt. This really helped me establish an underground club night in a very tough market. People used to flock from all over the South Coast for those gigs. They couldn't believe they'd paid £25 to see Carl at a rave like Sunrise the weekend before and here he was on the night they came to the club playing for £4. That was thirty years ago, and here we are in a scene where crowds are fickle and sounds and genres are constantly changing, with new and fresh DJs coming through all the time, but no one has ever been able to come close to what Carl has achieved and is continuing to achieve.

His popularity just increases every year, and for good reason - an event with Carl Cox is a guaranteed roadblock and his consistency behind the decks means he turns up every time and smashes it with his unmatched stage presence and positivity that just spreads through the crowd, whipping them into a frenzy night after night. He's a joy to watch and a joy to be around. As a DJ you can learn so much from him; he makes it look so easy despite being so technically brilliant. The only thing you find difficult as a DJ is coming on after him!

He is also the consummate professional, and all DJs and performers alike should aspire to have the work ethic of Carl. He is living proof that having such a long and successful career is based on being a genuinely nice person, being filled with a sheer talent and coupled with a passion for what he loves. One look at Carl and you can see that success can never be based on hype, ego and diva demands.

I count myself very lucky and privileged to have known Carl for close to thirty-five years. We've played on some amazing stages and clubs around the world together, including being a part of his incredible sixteen-year Space Ibiza legacy. We've shared many magical moments at dinners, in airports and on long car journeys, where the conversation is always full of loads of funny stories, smiles and laughs.

I count Carl as a true friend and am honoured to have been asked to write a few words for this book. His story is one of a DJ legend who has been there from the start of the whole culture and who continues to be instrumental in shaping the scene into the worldwide scene it is today. Carl shows us that hard work and drive go hand in hand with fun and laughter - he is one big bundle of happy. More than anything, though, Carl's story is about music and will inspire everyone to keep on dancing.

John Digweed,
London 2020

20.

Just One More!

So here we are.

The lights are on and the sound is off. But I couldn't resist jumping back in for one last little bit. This is the point where the club is trying to get everyone out and the staff want to close up but then they realise that the DJ and the crowd have become one as another 'very' last tune is played.

It is amazing to see how the dance music industry has grown. When it was a little scene with a handful of artists and promoters I could see that here was potential for our movement to become something, but I couldn't imagine how big it would get. I thought that by '94 or '95 we'd be done. Over. Finished. Kaput. Yet here we are in the 2020s and we're still going strong, bigger than ever! It's bloody awesome that we are still going and have become an unstoppable force. All because we came together!

I feel honoured that I've had the chance to share some of what makes me the person I am with you. Coming to the end of this isn't easy - I've really enjoyed the chance to reflect on some of the things that I've experienced so far. I have always tried to live for the moment. I've always thought that when things are bad they will get better and when things are good they should be enjoyed while they last. Maybe that's where my trademark smile comes from.

My record box is still full, and we've a lot more fun to have together, but for now this is it.

You don't have to go home but you can't stay here.

See you back on the dancefloor soon.

Oh yes, oh yes!

From Raves to Faves

When I was at school, I struggled to apply myself. I was so focused on playing music that nothing else mattered. Writing an essay was painful and I chewed my way through a lot of pens. Writing a book is different. It's been fun. I must admit that getting going wasn't easy but, once I got into it, it went from being work to being something that I couldn't wait to get back to. I feel a bit sad that this part of the process is drawing to a close.

What I thought I'd do is leave a few lists here. I've always liked finding out what other people like, so I figured that as you're reading about me you might want to know about some of the things that have moved and motivated me, and some of the people, places and moments that have helped shape me.

The first list of great dance music moments has had lots of input from people in the industry as well as bystanders who have followed the scene from afar. The rest of the lists are my personal choices, my opinion based on what I know I like and what I remember. If I've missed anything or anyone out then apologies, but I think these are pretty accurate. So before I change my mind again, here are some great:

- Dance Music Moments
- Tunes
- Bands
- DJs
- Clubs
- Cars & Bikes

MAKING MAGIC

50 Special Dance Music Moments

Dance music continues to give us so much. It nurtures emotions and relationships and inspires creativity all while bringing people together. We all have our favourite moments and have had those special times, some legendary and some less so, but all important none the less. And I'm sure there are many more magical moments yet to come that will help define electronic music and dance culture in the future.

After speaking to lots of people and discounting negative things that shaped the scene at the time like the Criminal Justice Act, the tragic ecstasy-related death of Leah Betts and the aftermath of the Castlemorton rave, alongside difficult but important moments like the impact of Avicii's death, I'm pretty happy with this list, especially as I've made it onto once or twice. Looking at the list, there are some obvious things that you'd expect to see here but are not here, like Stormzy head-lining at Glastonbury in his Banksy-designed stab-proof vest, D:Ream's 'Things Can Only Get Better' helping the Labour Party win a general election, David Guetta's conquering of America leading to the meteoric rise of EDM in the USA, and global superstars like Madonna being remixed by the likes of William Orbit, but you could say that these things, and many others, came about by the actions of trailblazers before them.

MDMA isn't on the list. We all know that the humble E played a part in shaping the scene, especially in the early acid house days, but explaining the impact of the disco biscuit in a list doesn't explain the highs and lows and the ups and downs. Also not on the list are lasers, smoke machines, flyers, turbo sound rigs and the other elements that helped shape the movement. Obviously, the Technics decks have to make it in.

Different electronic music styles are represented but the list is focused on electronic music rather than some of the genres based on the more traditional live instrument set-up, otherwise Eddie Piller launching Acid Jazz and Gilles Peterson's Talkin' Loud at Dingwalls would be on the list too. Important moments that elevated the dance scene – like when the Grammy Awards created the Remixer of the Year Award in 1998, which was won by Frankie Knuckles, and when they (finally) introduced the Best Electronic/Dance Album category in 2005 – are left off as they are a part of the evolution of the scene that became an industry.

I've also left out most references to recorded music, even though the impact and in some cases shockwaves were far-reaching. S'Express, the Shamen's 'Ebeneezer Goode' and Prodigy's 'Smack My Bitch Up' aren't here, but Underworld's explosive 'Born Slippy' from *Trainspotting*, the beautiful 'Unfinished Sympathy' from Massive Attack and Moby's album *Play* that had every track licensed for advertising and so reached a massive global prime-time audience are on the list.

Enough about what's not on the list. These are places you'd want to have been to, events you'd have wanted to be at, moments you'd have wanted to witness and pieces of music that may have touched your heart.

OH YES, OH YES!

The fifty special electronic music moments, in no particular order, are:

1. Closing party at David Mancuso's Loft
2. Kraftwerk perform at Tribal Gathering '97
3. Paul Oakenfold opens Spectrum
4. Moby releases *Play*
5. Ibiza Four experience Alfredo at Amnesia
6. U2 book Oakenfold to support their Zooropa Tour
7. Fatboy Slim performs to 250,000 people on Brighton Beach
8. Orbital live at Glastonbury '94
9. The Prodigy play live for Universe
10. Belleville Three come together in Detroit and 'invent' techno
11. Underworld release 'Born Slippy'
12. The birth of the Three Deck Wizard at Sunrise
13. Tiësto enters the arena and plays at the Athens Olympic Games and his stadium gig at Arnhem's GelreDome
14. Dr Motte's birthday party launches the Berlin Love Parade
15. Carl Cox and Paul Oakenfold play B2B at Stonehenge in 2018
16. Layo, Bushwaka! and Mr. C at The End
17. Carl Cox's long-running residency at Space in Ibiza
18. Goldie and Metalheadz at Blue Note
19. Paul Oakenfold's legendary Goa Mix for the *Essential Mix*
20. Frankie Knuckles DJing at the Warehouse
21. Massive Attack record 'Unfinished Sympathy'
22. Pete Tong launches the *Essential Mix* on BBC Radio 1 in '93
23. Chemical Brothers at the Sunday Social

24. Opening night at Danny Rampling's Shoom (Klub Sch-oom)
25. The KLF perform live at Spectrum
26. Chris Sullivan opens the WAG in the heart of London's West End
27. Soul II Soul at the Africa Centre
28. Rusty Egan DJing electronic music at the Blitz
29. Fabio and Grooverider bring us Rage
30. Nicky Holloway launches The Trip
31. Disco Donnie's US warehouse parties
32. Technics introduces the SL-1200 turntable in 1972
33. Sasha at Shelleys Laserdome
34. Junior Vasquez at the Sound Factory
35. Carl Cox's double New Year's Eve 1999 sets in Australia and Hawaii
36. Manumission Motel launches with the 'Lost Weekend'
37. Gary Haisman shouting 'Acieeed' at the Raid
38. Craig Richards' long running residency at Fabric
39. Irvine Welsh's *Trainspotting* hits the cinemas
40. Fabi Paras plays at Love Ranch
41. London's pirate radio station Kiss FM gets a licence
42. Larry Levan DJing at the Paradise Garage
43. Boy's Own's rave in '88 – the one with the geese on the lake
44. The Energy raves in '88 and '89
45. Laurent Garnier's five-hour set at Ultra in Miami
46. Mike Pickering and Graeme Park at the Hacienda
47. Sasha & John Digweed at Twilo, New York
48. Ministry of Sound opens its doors and the super-club is born
49. Nicky Siano plays Donna Summer's 'I Feel Love' at the Gallery in NYC, 1977
50. Perfecto Fluoro free party '95 in Ibiza

TOP TUNES

Music has made my life complete and I've worked hard to push boundaries musically. Most music can be defined by a style or genre, and it's rare to hear something that you can't explain. But that's what happened to me in 1986 when I first heard 'Acid Tracks' by DJ Pierre's Phuture. My mind was already open to experimental sounds, but this blew a big hole in my senses and I've been filling the gap with new beats and melodies ever since.

Every year I come across lots of great new music. Some of it is fresh out of the studio and sometimes it's a hidden gem on a B-side or a funk rarity that gets my smile going. I'm really into live electronic music and there is some amazing stuff being produced, so when I'm lucky enough to have access to something hotter than hot I try to work it into my sets. None of these tracks are on this short list. I've also left off anything that I've written, recorded, produced or remixed.

One electronic track on here has an extra-special meaning for me. I received a white label from DJ Rolando with a track called 'Knights of the Jaguar'. Receiving a track in the mail wasn't unusual; what made this stand out before I listened to it was the handwritten note from Rolando to me personally, asking me to give it a listen and that he thought I'd like it. I was curious and put it on, only to be instantly blown away. Perfection will do that to you. For a piece of techno, this record is exceptional. The emotions it generates make it so special, I've seen people crying on the dancefloor when I play it. I've been close once or twice too. It's so lovingly produced and cleverly put together, this is one of those tracks that once you hear it you can't help but feel uplifted.

The list here is music that means something to me. Each of these tunes is not just an awesome track but takes me back to a place, a time or a moment that helped define who I am. Everything started in my parents' front room, where I fell in love with some of the greatest bands and artists of all time, and this love affair has never ended. Some of my favourite bands have many amazing tracks but haven't made the list, so nothing here from the likes of Slave, the Beatles, Cameo, War, Fred Wesley & the J.B.'s and the Prodigy. I could have made a whole list just from Stevie Wonder's work. Most of the tunes here are not electronic but show my funk, soul and disco roots. There's nothing particularly specialist here either, just great pieces of music that lift my soul. Enjoy!

So, listed in alphabetical order are these beauties:

1. Aretha Franklin – Rock Steady
2. Art of Noise – Moments in Love
3. Ashford and Simpson – Don't Cost You Nothing
4. Average White Band – Pick up the Pieces
5. B.T. Express – Give Up the Funk
6. Barry White – Let the Music Play
7. Change – Paradise
8. Cheryl Lynn – Got to Be Real
9. Chic – São Paulo
10. Chuck Berry – No Particular Place to Go
11. Crown Heights Affair – Dancin'
12. David Bowie – Golden Years
13. Deodato – Night Cruiser

14.   Diana Ross – Love Hangover

15.   DJ Rolando – Knights of the Jaguar

16.   Donald Byrd – Wind Parade

17.   Donna Summer – I Feel Love

18.   Earth, Wind & Fire – Fantasy

19.   Frankie Knuckles – Move your Body

20.   Gary Numan – Cars

21.   Ingram – Mi Sabrina Tequana

22.   James Brown – Get Up Offa That Thing

23.   Jamiroquai – Starchild

24.   Joe Smooth – Promised Land

25.   KC and the Sunshine Band – Shake Your Booty

26.   LTJ Bukem – Music

27.   Mandrill – Can You Get It

28.   Marvin Gaye – I Heard It through the Grapevine

29.   Mass Production – Welcome to Our World (of Merry Music)

30.   Massive Attack – Unfinished Sympathy

31.   Maze featuring Frankie Beverly – Twilight

32.   Melba Moore – You Stepped into My Life

33.   Michael Jackson – Rock with You

34.   New Order – Blue Monday

35.   Roy Ayers – Running Away

36.   Stevie Wonder – Pastime Paradise

37.   The Bar-Kays – Holy Ghost

38.   The Blackbyrds – Rock Creek Park

39.   The Police – Spirits in the Material World

40.   Wilson Pickett – In the Midnight Hour

A FEW BANDS

Having put together a list of some of my favourite tunes, I thought I'd better put a few of my favourite bands down. This isn't easy, as I've always loved albums, and I thought I'd restrict this list to twenty bands only. Originally, buying an album was a way for me to get a few singles on one piece of vinyl, but when I started to listen to the tracks I hadn't heard of I'd start to get a feeling of what the artists were trying to achieve. As my DJ life got going albums made way for singles, but when I started travelling listening to entire albums became part of the trip and it was a way to really get to understand a band's work.

In this list I've tried to steer away from bands where there is an obvious front person, even when the band are all excellent, so no James Brown & the J.B.'s or Prince & the Revolution, but I have included Goldie, as his albums are very collaborative with other artists alongside the Metalheadz. On the opposite side of the coin, some bands like Queen are amazing as a unit but it took the power of Freddie Mercury's personality and voice to make Queen the band it was.

I love all these bands for different reasons, but love them I do. With an A–Z line-up I give you:

1.   The Beatles
2.   Blondie
3.   The Brand New Heavies
4.   The Chemical Brothers
5.   Chic

6. The Clash
7. Daft Punk
8. Destiny's Child
9. Duran Duran
10. Earth, Wind & Fire
11. Goldie
12. The Isley Brothers
13. Kraftwerk
14. Limp Bizkit
15. Massive Attack
16. New Order
17. The Prodigy
18. Queen
19. Soul II Soul
20. Underworld

LOVE THESE DJS

I'm often asked who my favourite DJ is. The person asking normally looks a little nervous, a bit as if by recommending 'the competition' I could be lowering my own worth. Ridiculous! I love hearing other DJs, especially when I can relax, listen and learn. I'm very fortunate that I get to play with so much diverse talent on different bills. From my own events to ones where I am a guest and from tiny clubs to major festivals, I get to share what I love with people who also love what they do.

I've had lots of influences along the way, like Trevor Fung and Froggy in the early days when I was learning about the differences between keeping a club crowd going until 2am versus rocking a school disco until 9pm. There are even some of the early rave DJs whose names I didn't catch and who I never saw or heard from again but who left me with a little bit of inspiration.

I've shared a bill with everyone on my list and loved rocking out to their own distinctive sound. Each of them brings something special when they play. Different styles of playing and different styles of music, but all of them are bloody fantastic.

This lot are all great and 100 per cent in alphabetic order. You should try to enjoy them whenever you get the chance. My dancefloor champions:

1. Adam Beyer
2. Andy C
3. Dave Clarke

4.   Jamie Jones
5.   Jeff Mills
6.   John Digweed
7.   Joseph Capriati
8.   Josh Wink
9.   Laurent Garnier
10. Loco Dice
11. Maceo Plex
12. Marco Carola
13. Miss Djax
14. Monika Kruse
15. Nic Fanciulli
16. Nicole Moudaber
17. Pan-Pot
18. Sasha
19. Sven Väth
20. Tiësto

KINGS OF CLUBS

My home from home. I've spent so much time in clubs that it's like having a second home, and playing all over the world has meant that I have many places I feel comfortable in. Every time I play - from a club to a rave, and a festival to a gathering - is special, but there are some club venues that stand out in my mind and give me goose bumps when I think of them.

This can be for a whole bunch of reasons. Normally it starts with the sound system (like any craftsman I like to have the best tools at my disposal) but then it all boils down to one thing, the atmosphere. The atmosphere itself is a combination of two things: how the crowd reacts to me and how I react to the crowd. This combination can make a party electric.

Putting together a list of clubs is tricky, because I've played at so many excellent venues. This list is based on some of my best experiences, so there's a healthy UK presence, although there are clubs across nine different countries. On a list like this the Zap in Brighton can sit alongside DC10 in Ibiza, which is part of what clubbing is all about - you make your memories wherever you are. I've played with friends, for friends and made friends at the clubs on this list. I've only listed clubs I've actually played at, otherwise a list of great clubs would have to include the Warehouse, Paradise Garage, Studio 54 and the Loft.

So here are twenty clubs, listed alphabetically, that have had or continue to have an impact on me:

OH YES, OH YES!

1. Beta – Denver, USA
2. Cavo Paradiso – Mykonos, Greece
3. Cream – Liverpool, UK
4. DC10 – Ibiza, Spain
5. Fabric – London, UK
6. Hacienda – Manchester, UK
7. Le Rex Club – Paris, France
8. Limelight – New York, USA
9. Motor – Detroit, USA
10. Omen – Frankfurt, Germany
11. Renaissance – Nottingham, UK
12. Space – Ibiza, Spain
13. The End – London, UK
14. Twilo – New York, USA
15. Velvet Underground – London, UK
16. Warung Beach Club – Santa Catarina, Brazil
17. WHP – Manchester, UK
18. Womb – Tokyo, Japan
19. Zap Club – Brighton, UK
20. Zouk Club – Singapore

CARS AND BIKES

Motorsport has become a big part of my life, so it makes sense for me to share some dream machines with you. I love anything to do with the Mini - I have felt that way since I first saw *The Italian Job* - and I'm really into drag racing as a spectator and a driver. I'm a fan of bikes with sidecars and still have a soft spot for my old scooter with its 'L' plates. I could go on and on, but instead I thought I would only include individual vehicles that are super-special in their own unique way.

So for the petrolheads, the lovers of speed, design gurus and for people who just like looking at beautiful things, I give you, in no particular order, my dream list:

20 Cars

1. Mk 1 Lotus Cortina
2. 2004 Ford GT
3. Jaguar E-Type
4. Mercedes – 560 SEC
5. Lancia Delta Integrale Evo III
6. Porsche Carrera GT
7. Ferrari Enzo 2002
8. Ariel Atom
9. Pagani Zonda
10. Honda NSX
11. Porsche GT3 RS

12.   Bugatti Veyron
13.   Ford Mustang Bullitt 67
14.   Volvo – P1800
15.   McLaren F1
16.   Ford Escort Mexico Mk1
17.   Citroën DS
18.   Corvette Stingray C2 1964
19.   Dodge Charger 1968
20.   Aston Martin DB5

10 Bikes

1.   MV Agusta – 675 Serie Oro
2.   Suzuki RG500 Gamma
3.   Honda RCV 213
4.   Suzuki Hayabusa
5.   Yamaha LC RD 350
6.   Honda RC 30
7.   Yamaha FS1 E 50cc
8.   Kawasaki Z900
9.   Ducati Desmosedici RR
10.   Harley Davidson – V-Rod

Thank You!

Without a whole bunch of people supporting me and creating opportunities for me my life would have been very different. I couldn't end this book without handing out a giant high five. Scrap that. Let's make it big tens.

Now, where do I start?

I've talked a lot about family in this book and I have to start by sharing this moment with my late parents: my father, Henry Carlisle Cox, and my beloved mother, Patricia. Your boy done good!

Big shout-out to my sisters Andrea and Pamela and my niece Rhianna for their never-ending love and support. It has been a hard year for us but we have been able to stay close and connected. Family first. Love you guys.

Ian Hussey, you're a star. We've had some adventures, and then some. You're the king of the tour managers, making my life a lot easier. Your support and loyalty on and off the road is invaluable. I'm sure I don't thank you enough, but you know I am very grateful for everything you do.

A special thank you to my friend and manager Alon Shulman, without whom this book wouldn't have happened. Alon, you are the master at connecting the dots and making the impossible possible. Thank you and the team at World Famous Promotions for all you do. With so much on the horizon for us, I also have to reach out to the Shulman crew, Samantha, Felix, Lara and Serena, for being part of our adventure.

Ian Hindmarsh: we've been through so much and I thank you for putting me in the right places at the right time and helping me share my vision around the world. You've taken me to places I could never have dreamed of and it's been a wild ride, with more adventures to come. A big thank you to you, Tara, Michelle and the whole Analog family.

My wonderful friend Pepe Rosello, you saw something in me and believed that we could do something special together and we did. Pure magic was created at Space in Ibiza, but none of this would have been possible without you believing in me. *Muchas gracias por todo.*

With no rule book or career path I have to be eternally grateful to Maxine Bradshaw, Lynn Cosgrave, Paul Morris, Rachel Birchwood and Rachel Turner, who came into my life at different key points and who all helped me gain recognition as a DJ and grow as a person. You believed in me, fought for me and shaped my journey, helping make me the artist I am today. It isn't possible here to show how much I appreciate all the great things you helped me achieve, but I will always be very grateful.

Thank you and huge respect for your kind words to Laurent Garnier and John Digweed. You are among the finest DJs that the scene has produced, proven by your longevity and the love for what you do. I am very lucky that dance music has given me friends like you.

The rave scene was a big part of what got me to where I am. We came together as one and, united, we pushed dance music out far and wide. This list can never be complete but Big Love to all the DJs, promoters, MCs and all the rave family, including: DJ Ratty, Seduction, Jumping Jack Frost, Fabio, Grooverider, Colin Dale, Tintin, the Energy Crew, Anton Le

THANK YOU!

Pirate, Mickey Finn, Parks & Wilson, Slipmatt, Westbam, A Guy Called Gerald, Seal, Adamski, Bam Bam, Joey Beltram, Helter Skelter, Dreamscape, Genesis, C.J. Bolland, Guru Josh, Raindance, ESP, Universe, 808 State, Bandulu, Altern-8, Trevor Fung, Shut Up and Dance, Ragga Twins, Rebel MC, Dave Clarke, SL2, Ratpack, Shades of Rhythm, N-Joi, 2 Bad Mice, Top Buzz, Mr. OZ, Top Cat, Mr. C, K-Klass, Brisk, Dougal, Hixxy, Randall, Underground Resistance, Reel II Reel, Judge Jules, Insomnia, Hype, Prodigy, Nicky Blackmarket, the Panda Van, DJ SS, Bryan G, Kenny Ken, Swan E, Colin Hudd, Graeme Park, Phantasy, Trevor Rockcliffe, Robbi Dee, Magika, Energetic, Lyndon C, Rendezvous, Stacey Tough, Stu Allen, Pete Heller, Jim Masters, DJ Rap, Easygroove, Steve Dare, Sunrise, John Kelly, Joe Peng, Pigbag, Amnesia House, Billy Nasty, Eddie Richards, MC Pure Love, Colin Faver, Tribal Gathering, Telepathy, MC Ribbs, LTJ Bukem, Clarkee, Frankie Bones, Pandemonium, Nipper, Fantazia and the convoys plus the hundreds of thousands of ravers who carried the whole scene forward and turned our little secret ('Oi! Oi!') into a world of lifelong friendships and global domination.

The original crew from the Carshalton and Brighton days – always in my thoughts – Leeroy James, Milton Jones, Dave Kilmurry, Ray Locke, Paul Burgess, Mark Hagerty, Jim Mason, David Carter, Karen Caiger and Gary Hicks.

Big moments deserve big thanks, so I'd like to acknowledge the special atmosphere created by Dr Motte and the Love Parade crew, all the original ravers, everyone that was involved in Space across all those seasons, the Carl and Eric's Mobile Disco massive, the Pure crew, everyone involved in *Cabin Fever – the Vinyl Sessions*, the Burning Man team who make the Playground so unique, and every single Burner out on the *playa*.

Carl Cox Motorsport might have my name on the tin, but we are a big family. Colin Buckley, Robbie Shorter, Tracey and Steve Bryan, Barry Smith, Tim Reebes, Mark Wilkes, Michael and Ben Neeves, Michael Dunlop, Jo and Jonathan Gauci, Frank Marchese, Gary Shepherd, Harley Stephens, Andrew Nissan, Matt Carey, Rod Taylor, Dave the Sparky, Bruce Antsy, Davey Todd, Connor Cummins, Clive Padgett, the Isle of Man TT team and Mike Edwards - you all rock. And the London Motor Show team: Alon, Alec and Kim.

I'm lucky to work with some very talented people in the studio and across the labels, so a big thank you to my partner at Awesome Soundwave Christopher Coe, and also Steve Ward, Neil McLellan, Jon Rundell, everyone at Awesome Soundwave and everyone at Intec. Excited about the next chapter with Matt King, Korda Marshall, Lisa Wilkinson and the team at BMG behind me. Big thanks to all my collaborators and the artists who have trusted me to remix and produce them. Huge respect to Nile Rodgers for putting the 'fun' into funk.

I've played with so many great artists and couldn't possibly name you all here, but I must shout out some of the people who've joined me on the ride. Some of them go way back to the rave days and some are new friends. Thank you for what you've shared and the fun we've had - looking forward to many more good times. A big Carl hug goes out to John Digweed, Norman Jay, Paul Oakenfold, Pete Tong, Terry Farley, Eats Everything, Ralph Lawson, Mark Lewis, Sven Väth, Monika Kruse, Josh Wink, Eric Powell, Laurent Garnier, Darren Emerson, everyone at Pure, Liam Howlett, Danny Rampling, Jeff Mills, Richie Hawtin, Paul and Phil Hartnoll the Orbital boys, Charlotte de Witte, Norman Cook aka Fatboy Slim, Jim Masters, Dave Beer, the Chemical Brothers, Dave

Angel, Aubrey, Sasha, Mike and Claire Manumission, Moby, Mark Moore, Alfredo, Adam Beyer, Andy C, Dave Clarke, Jamie Jones, Joseph Capriati, Loco Dice, Marco Carola, Miss Djax, Nic Fanciulli, Nicole Moudaber, Pan-Pot and Tiësto.

Thank you for supporting me on the journey: Lina Kotzian, Phillip Straub, Dan Tait, Judy Higgins, Richard Rees-Pulley, Dave Browning, Sarah Sparta, Eoin Smyth, Jeroen Bosschers, Tina Browning, Sara Cooper, Julien Toriannare, Vittoria Pela, Roman Trystram, Cynthia Kummer, Rick de la Croix, Zenith, Ruben Mira Blanco, Fritz Pangratz, Angeline Smirnoff, Pablo Hassan, Grant Best, Mark Grotefeld, Newell Lock, Deborah Parsons, Phil Burgin, Pioneer DJ, Game Over Ibiza, *chef patron* Andy Needham, Ben Turner, Alli Pratt, Sensorium, Dan Reid, Steve Rose, Jim Baggott, Russell Faibisch, Richie McNeil, Carl Loben, Nick Stevenson, Fraser Boyes, Lee Brackstone at White Rabbit, Jo Whitford, Ian Allen and Sophie Hicks.

I've had the pleasure of connecting with so many people and making some great friendships. Many have been acknowledged here already but I'd also like to show some love and respect to Mark Ferguson, Russell Small, Antony Denness, Purve, Tim The Taxi, Steve Maddog, Nifty, Rod The Fixer, Big Rob, Paul Wells, Phillip Rosa, Gary Barnes (RIP), Toni Palmer, Johan & Anja, Raymondo, Steffen Charles, Marco Bailey, Charles Barthelemy, Jim Barden and Steve King.

If you feel I've missed you out then I probably have so even though it's not the same I want everyone whose been a positive part of my life so far to share in the love and friendship I feel for you all.

My heart. If you want to live your life by one lyric you couldn't do much better than 'All you need is love'. Some people are special and I'm lucky to have you in my life. You know who you are! You're creative, driven and help produce the best in me. Having come through those tough times with such courage is an inspiration to me. Big Smile!

My fans. I started with a handful of followers and am now very lucky to have such a massive global fanbase. We share a love of music and of connecting through the energy across the dancefloor. You keep pushing me to push myself and I thank you, my fans and fans of dance culture and electronic music, from the bottom of my heart for so much love and support.

Finally, I want to thank a young Carl Andrew Cox for believing in yourself and what you felt you could accomplish. You never gave up. You struggled to get yourself going. You were determined to never give up and follow your dreams. You didn't waver from your course. You always kept your dreams alive. Your dreams became my reality. I'm proud of you.

Carl Cox always wanted to share his love of music with others, and the 'Three Deck Wizard' quickly became 'The People's Choice' of the emerging rave scene. He has gone on to become one of the most globally renowned electronic music artists, winning countless accolades, including a record thirty-four consecutive *DJ Mag* nominations since the awards began in 1998. Continuously performing as a headline DJ and live act worldwide, creating in the studio where he is a prolific remixer and recording artist, or behind the wheel at the race track with his motorsports team, Carl is known for pushing boundaries and breaking down barriers. He's settled in Melbourne, Australia, but feels at home wherever there is a dancefloor.

Alon Shulman is a promoter, artist manager and award-winning producer. Founder of the World Famous Group, he acts as special advisor to individuals and organisations and continues to 'make the impossible possible'. Passionate about everything that makes up the global events industry, he has hosted over 400 of the world's finest DJs and electronic live acts at his own shows, including Paul Oakenfold and Carl Cox at Stonehenge. He is the author of several books, including *The Second Summer of Love*. He lives in London with his wife and three children.